A LEADER IN
THE MIRROR

A LEADER IN THE MIRROR:

Revealing the Leader in You!

Joel Parker

JONES MEDIA
PUBLISHING

A Leader in the Mirror: Revealing the Leader in You! Copyright © 2018 by Joel Parker.

Jones Media Publishing
10645 N. Tatum Blvd. Ste. 200-166
Phoenix, AZ 85028
www.JonesMediaPublishing.com

Printed in the United States of America

ISBN: ISBN-13: 978-1-945849-56-5 paperback

DEDICATION

Dedicated to my family–Linda, Sarah and Preston
for their inspiration and support.

In memory of my Daddy and Mother James
D. Parker and Roberta J. Parker my heroes and
life long supporters.

In memory of my Father in Law Larry W.
Houtz friend and encourager through the
best and worst of times.

CONTENTS

Acknowledgements

THE INSPIRATION OF THIS BOOK came after years of consulting for my wife as she grew a thriving business. I want to thank my beautiful wife, Linda Parker, not only for her support and encouragement but also for her modeling a servant leader. She more than inspired me to write this book, she also implemented many of the principles and models presented here into her leadership practices through the years. This allowed me to develop and validate these ideas before I shared them with others.

As the manuscript was being developed it would have never been transformed into a viable book without the help of Dr. Phillip Patterson and Christine Moore. It is a brutal process to have your work critically edited but their professionalism and expertise proved to be invaluable in my maturation as a writer.

I would also like to thank Melissa Boeger and Mary Wright for their time and instructive feedback. Melissa and Mary are experienced leaders and have achieved and flourished in more than one career. They have both had amazing personal and professional journeys and their insight helped me fine tune the message.

Finally, I want to thank my mother, Roberta Parker, who passed from this earth in 2012 but had significant influence on this book. Mother was a reporter, researcher and writer who helped me formulate and express my story when it was bottled up deep within me. I will never forget the time she told me "you should write a book someday."

CHAPTER 1:
WHAT A SHAMBLES!

I SAT IN MY CAR at a park near my house—tears in my eyes, Bible in hand, praying. I normally love the fall with its refreshing air, football talk on sports radio, and normalcy after everyone returns home after vacations. But this fall was different: at 29 I found myself financially devastated and no hope in sight. What started out as an exciting business venture had ended in total disaster.

Instead of having a full workday ahead, I had nowhere to go and didn't know what to do. I would return to that park day after day for weeks, delving into my Bible. As a Christian, I knew of multiple stories of redemption in the Bible and I was searching for any that would correlate with my current situation. As I studied and prayed, I still remember thinking how inconceivable it was that I could work my way out of this mess. And I was right: *I* could not work my way out of this mess. I needed faith that God would guide me through the darkness.

I started out grappling with the instincts of fight, flight, or freeze. What was I capable of in such a time of desperation? Thoughts invaded my consciousness. Negative feelings came over me: anger, bitterness, and hopelessness. I was so paralyzed that the only thing I could do was to literally just wake up and start each day and do that one day at a time. Each day the same: get up and try to do something constructive.

Over the weeks as I prayed, studied, and thought, I began to feel an increasing sense of boldness, determination, and hope. Gradually, a peace set over me. I held tight to family, church, and friends. I became distinctly aware of God guiding me, which of course, He had been doing all along. I had to combine faith with my actions. While I still needed to plan and be productive, I also needed to understand I was not the mastermind here.

Looking back, I can see that everything that happened contributed to God's purpose for my life. I always had a latent confidence and ambition. However, I was hoping God would lay out an opportunity in front of me to make me wildly successful. What I didn't realize was that I wasn't ready to be wildly successful. **I wasn't that person - yet.**

As far back as high school, I was an astute observer and follower, always waiting to see what I was supposed to do next and looking for opportunities that others would give me. When I dated, it was because a girl expressed interest in me. When I tried out for the select soccer team, it was because the coach asked me. When I got a job, it was because someone referred me. Inside, I recognized and was uncomfortable with this passivity, and I would occasionally show flashes of ambition and initiative, but nothing consistent.

When I received my degree in Construction Science from the School of Architecture at the University of Oklahoma, I looked for jobs that employers would "give" me. True to form, I took the safest bet, staying on with a construction company where I interned. It turned out to be a good job with opportunities for growth. I quickly moved into management and reported directly to the president. My department developed new home designs along with estimating material needs and costs.

I was fulfilling my dream of designing homes and grew to know intimately the construction business and managing people. I had a leadership position and was poised to leverage my creative and analytical strengths. I thought to myself: 'this has to be God's purpose for my life.'

Over the next few years the company grew substantially, and I realized how impactful and difficult it was being a leader. I realized that leadership had more to do with the person and not the position. *And, the path of observing and following others was going to lead to a life of observing and following others as they fulfilled their dreams, not mine.* I respected and learned from the company leaders, and I became more assertive and sure of myself.

However, things began to change as the company expanded and had to adapt. The owners could no longer lead with just their personalities, and they seemed to struggle leading in situations where they were not in direct control. I started to see the consequences of leaders not understanding how to lead beyond the authority of their position. I felt the agony of leaders losing their cool. My fate was in the hands of others who I hoped were making good decisions and executing them at a high level.

As time went on, it became apparent that neither of these were happening.

Most of us have felt the frustration when leadership doesn't understand or respect the people in an organization—especially in tough times. Eventually, I was asked to do things that we didn't have the capacity to do. Ethical lines began to blur as we needed to put on a good show for stakeholders. This was coming from good men who I respected but were buckling just when we needed strong leadership.

Key employees left. Most of them started their own companies. My wife, Linda, had been working at the company as a successful sales manager. However, we didn't feel comfortable having both our careers dependent on one company. She left to become the real estate sales manager for a former colleague who started his own company. Shortly thereafter, I quit pursuing my MBA, left the company, and formed my own company designing and building homes.

In hindsight, I realize how ill-prepared I was to make this move. I started by contracting with former associates. Then I began to branch out and grow my business network. It was invigorating running my own business, and there were successes. There were also challenges. I still did not understand how to be a good leader. I resisted the mentorship and advice of those with more experience. I did not comprehend the effort it required to be successful. My problems were solvable, and I eventually found my mentor, but soon thereafter we discovered Linda was pregnant with our first child. This spawned an important realization: the industry I was in was a poor fit for my ambitions. We decided I should find a new career

One of the things I didn't learn in business school is how to transition *out* of business. We thought we had a good financial plan as I transitioned to a new career. But our process to carefully disassemble our company and ease into our new life turned into a demolition job rife with looters. I lost focus and control. Those we thought we could trust proved to be untrustworthy. We ended up broke; worse than broke, we owed money we didn't have.

So, after several months, there I was in my car; Bible in my hands, praying that God would show mercy on me, my wife, and my newborn daughter. It didn't feel like it then, but looking back, God blessed me more than I deserved.

Without knowing it, through this trauma, I had actually gained the foundation and the tools I needed to be successful. I refer to this period as getting my Ph.D. in Life and Leadership. My "education" didn't comprise of post graduate classes. It was the whole experience of peaks and valleys in selecting mentors, taking risks, testing my character, understanding myself, and relying on teams that all added up to my development as a leader. While I've never stopped learning, God showed me in that car that I was now armed with the education and experience, and the clarity to apply them, which would be my catalyst for success.

When I desperately needed guidance and direction, God revealed a leader in me. I once looked in the mirror and loathed the man I saw for getting my family in this predicament. Then I began to see the man who would eventually lead his family forward in faith, prosperity, and charity.

I have since dedicated my career to understanding and sharing a leader's life. I have come to believe that leadership is the crux of what

> *There is more of a leader in you than you realize, but you just can't see them sometimes.*

you need to thrive personally and professionally, especially if you want to change your current situation. There is more of a leader in you than you realize, but you just can't see them sometimes. I want to share something from my insight and experience to help you see A Leader in the Mirror.

CHAPTER 2:
WHAT? I'M A LEADER?

WHAT I HOPE TO CONVEY in this book are the wonders of revealing the leader in you. Even if you have no ambition for leading large organizations, revealing your leadership can transform your life as you take control of your destiny. Leadership affects every aspect of your life. You can find benefit in leading yourself, your family, a large organization, a small company, a church group, or any team.

The study of leadership has a rich history, with many valuable theories, principles, models, and traits. There are also many great contemporary books on leadership. Amongst all this information I found one nugget that rings most true for me. Throughout history, people were seen as leaders as they learned to see and follow their own vision. Such is the interdependence of living in a society, that those who saw and followed their own vision affected others who were seeking direction. Today, the term "leadership" focuses on your influence over others, but it is rooted in leading yourself.

> *...if you're seeking personal growth as a leader, opportunities will find you.*

What I have learned on my journey is this: if you're seeking personal growth as a leader, opportunities will find you. Are you ready to notice those opportunities?

Do you currently hold a leadership position—either professionally, or in your community? Some people gain authority based solely on position or title—not on their ability to lead. This is probably the worst way to cultivate leadership skills, because it is easy to develop bad habits. Once you find yourself in a position of authority, people simply follow you because they have to. This makes it hard for you to realize which behavior is truly effective and which is not. When you try to act like a leader before you understand the leader in you, your leadership is vulnerable, especially in situations where you cannot use the influence of your position.

If you've ever found yourself saying, "Do you know who I am?" in an effort to command respect from someone, you are not demonstrating true leadership. You must learn who you are as a leader *in spite of* your position—not derive authority from it. Consider the list of positions below and think about how they might lend themselves to authority based on position versus being a good leader. It might help if you phrase this as, "just because you are a (an) _____ or have a (an) _____ doesn't mean you are inherently a good leader." Here are some leadership positions you might occupy:

- Company owner or founder

- Older, more tenured senior employee

- Parent

- Expert in your field

- Advanced degrees

- Wealthy

- Advanced intelligence

- Loudest

- Most outspoken

- Title or granted authority

- Personal accomplishments

Most of these positions *do* deserve respect. And these positions can *help you* become a worthy leader. However, they should not *define you* as a leader.

How is a Leader Defined?

On a trip to New York City, Linda and I were staying at a hotel that overlooked Times Square. One afternoon, we heard a great ruckus outside. We looked down and saw a parade of NASCAR cars turning the corner and driving by our hotel. Anyone could tell immediately that these cars were out of place with the commuters and taxi cabs. Later, we found out it was a promotional gig and they were going to park the cars along the curbs for photo ops. So, we went down to have a look. Although I'm not a NASCAR enthusiast, I appreciated the power and engineering that went into these machines.

I remember thinking driving a race car must be a grueling experience requiring extraordinary physical and mental stamina. The car interior—with harnesses, safety gear, gauges and switches in plain sight—testified to its rigor. It was not a car for a novice. Reflecting on this, I could tell that before a driver could compete at the highest levels, he or she must endure an enormous amount of preparation. In the same way, a leader is developing a group of people to emulate them. It is a scary thought for some of us, but you don't have to be perfect; you just have to be continually involved in growing personally to be a good **Leader**.

A professional race car driver also needs to develop a relationship with his or her car. It takes countless hours of work prior to race day to ensure a car is ready to drive and to win. I like to refer to the time "under the hood" or "behind the wheel" as **The Leader Effect**. While a driver may not be the one working on the mechanics, each knows what they like, what they want, and what is required for a winning strategy. They will ultimately be the ones to make sure everything is running well and will take control of the performance. Similarly, The Leader Effect is how someone is viewed as they take control of the team as the leader.

But it is not enough for the driver to be prepared and the car to be performing well. For the driver to be a champion they must consistently win. The driver has to assure excellence permeates throughout their staff and crew. **The Leader Legacy** is a Culture of Success, even where the leader is not directly involved.

To see the leader in you, there is a similar progression. You must first develop yourself personally and prepare yourself to lead others. Then, be seen being a leader. Prepare your team. Set expectations. Finally, influence your organization where there is an expectation for excellence.

Through my experiences, I have developed some processes that have proven beneficial in helping people reveal the leader in themselves. I like the frame of mind of seeing the leader in you. These processes don't magically turn you into a good leader, but they are practical steps to help you use your uniqueness to be a successful leader.

The fundamentals of the processes I devised came as I progressed through my professional life. Early on, when I owned the small residential design/build company, I managed a staff and crews of contractors. Then I led a team as a Senior Analyst and managed a sales team as a Sales Manager with Merck Pharmaceuticals. I later served as an executive of a small consulting firm. Then I founded a consulting firm with the intent of helping small businesses grow successful organizations.

As it turned out, my firm's primary client ended up being Linda when I worked with her as she developed a Network Marketing organization of one person into an organization of multiple teams and thousands of people representing over $60 million in annual revenue. Linda told me once that she wanted to build this business to generate a little extra income for our family. She ended up building a business that has given us financial independence and helps other people grow prosperous businesses.

Over the last several years, I have noticed a consistent culture in my work with Linda's organization that would be the envy of any organization. The professionalism, collaboration, integrity, and success of this group of people is unlike anything I've seen in any other organization. Any cases running counter to the culture are eventually rooted out organically. This book was inspired by a conversation I had with others that had partnered with their spouses in Linda's organization. Many of us, having resigned from promising corporate careers, realized that if our corporate organizations had had a culture like the one we enjoy now, it would have been difficult to leave our positions.

Originally, Linda did not set out to build a career in Network Marketing. But she was drawn to this particular company and was a loyal consumer of their quality products long before she started her business. Based on different experiences people have with this industry, it is important that you understand the company Linda's organization represents. It should be noted that I don't mention the name of the company because the focus here is on leadership and on not building a Network Marketing company. The company Linda's business is a distributor for began over three decades ago, to develop, manufacture, and market quality consumables.

This company is similar to traditional companies that produce consumable products, distribute through sales or wholesale organizations, and compensate their distributors based on volume of products sold. The difference is that our company distributes these personal use products through networks of independent representatives directly to clients instead of through advertising and retailing. Regardless of how the independent representative's organizations are structured, they are compensated on volume of products sold. Therefore, Linda had to develop an organization to move products to be successful.

Even with a quality company, product, and pay plan, success hinges on effective leadership. The sales force is made up entirely of independent representatives, where "employees" pick us instead of us "hiring" them. Management is developed through performance and leadership; there is no inherent, hierarchical authority. In this environment, a leader's position alone grants them very little authority. The title helps, but people will not align themselves with leaders unless they demonstrate strong leadership skills.

...one's title does not define true leadership.

In this company's compensation plan, independent representatives earn titles based on performance achievements. However, true success is in the line of leaders, not titles. Most corporate workers probably understand this; some executives wield power, while other executives are less respected. Most employees of traditional companies know who the experts are and who gets things done regardless of titles. In our organization, people know who they need to emulate or get advice from regardless of their title. And in all cases, one's title does not define true leadership.

Even though other people can give you a title, no one can make you a worthy leader; you find the leader in yourself, and people notice. Your organization will thrive if you continually develop yourself and everyone in your organization as leaders. I think there are many leadership lessons for corporate organizations in looking at an organization of independent representatives. We sometimes refer to it as leading a "volunteer army." I plan to tie in lessons from all types of organizations and develop principles for successful leadership that transcend all organization types and focus on you as a leader.

When I had done some serious life reflection in my car during the bad times, I realized how my own experiences could bolster my effectiveness as a leader. Later, when I heard hundreds of individuals in Linda's business tell their own fantastic, gut wrenching stories of personal transformation, I saw the love, hope, and service they provided to their teams. I knew that these people learned to lead through personal growth. I saw how others who develop their innate knack for leadership can guide others from any "position" in any organization – no matter where they are on an organization chart.

Emphasis on personal growth is a critical quality, not only for those who work as independent representatives, but also for those in a more traditional corporate organization. While personal growth might be more difficult in a corporate setting because you can have adequate performance without it, it is important in developing true leadership.

Most of the leaders in Linda's organization recognized things they needed to change about themselves before they could develop a team that would follow them. This is true for anyone who wants to lead others successfully: you need to continually spend time developing yourself, so people will want to follow you, not have to follow you.

Think of how much better the work environment would be if leaders worked on improving themselves – not merely getting people to do as they say.

Keep the race car in your mind as you look at three major themes in this book. The first is developing The Leader at a personal level: The race car driver preparing for the race. The second is The Leader Effect: The direct interaction with the car. The third is The Leader Legacy: The driver's influence in creating a Culture of Success.

In the following section, we'll focus on you, the leader, and your personal growth. This is where you will start to see the leader in yourself. However effective a leader you currently believe you are, it is important to **continually** strive for personal growth.

There's another type of driver that comes into play, and that's the getaway driver. It's likely that some of us have either witnessed or even been this driver before. This is the driver who stole a car they know very little about, and their only plan is to push on the gas. They take actions just to avoid crashing or getting caught. The race car driver is generally proactive in his/her driving, while the getaway driver is reactive.

Imagine a car chase scene from an action movie. It's a fun movie to watch but would become no fun if you were in the back seat and your life (or livelihood) depends on the outcome of the wild ride. You've all seen "leaders" who run their organizations like this. It's always wild but it usually ends with a crash.

One last thought:
Think about any area in your life that you want to have more success in or peace with. Now, think of yourself as the leader in making this happen. What would you do? Who do you need to be? No one has as much control of this situation as you do, as the leader.

Notes and Insights: Before you move forward, jot down some of your thoughts here. Don't put much time into thinking about it. These are first impressions of the chapter. Take the time to do this then read back over these notes later. You may be surprised by your own wisdom and insight. Do this after every chapter.

SECTION I: THE LEADER

The Leader: The person who leads; not necessary the one in the leadership position. The most important person you can lead is yourself. Purposefully develop yourself to be the leader you would want to follow.

CHAPTER 3:
HIERARCHY OF PERSONAL GROWTH

LINDA STARTED WORKING HER NETWORK Marketing business part time as a "side business" before I started my home design and construction business. She had become successful in new home sales and as a sales manager. As she worked her "side business" she would do just enough to earn incentive trips and first level promotion. Later, her checks would get smaller and she would lose her promotion as she focused energy on her real estate career. She repeated this process several times. However, she was destined to lead a large organization with her "side business" one day, but she was not yet the person to do that.

> *...you must prepare yourself before you can expect to succeed in leading others or leading an organization.*

Just like race car drivers prepare themselves to drive, you must prepare yourself before you can expect to succeed in leading others or leading an organization. In my journey, I developed a hierarchy of personal growth that I depend on to lead myself and others to success.

Level 1 – Focus on Personal Character

Regarding leadership, President Abraham Lincoln said that "...if you want to test a man's character, give him power." True, but this is not the best time to develop your own character. You can't wait until you are in a leadership position to understand your character. You must immediately embark on a continuous and purposeful endeavor to develop personal character.

For me, personal character – deciding what characteristics defined me, was truly foundational because I discovered that no matter what I said or did, people ultimately related to me based on my character. Character may not be the most charismatic aspect of leadership, but it is the most emotionally binding one. Most of us want to be known as a good person. When that sentiment is validated by a decision to deem someone as their leader, a strong bond is forged. People may be drawn to your intelligence, charisma, legacy, title, or talent, but it is your character that binds people to you.

More importantly, character is what binds you to the most important person that you need to influence as a leader ... you! This bond creates consistency. Besides you and God, no one really knows your true character. Don't let inconsistent character be a barrier to your personal growth. The important thing to note is that in your journey to instill good character in yourself, you can start as late as ... right now! I have learned this from personal experience and through seeing others develop into great leaders.

There are three steps to becoming the person of character you need to be.

1. Forgive yourself. I am sure most of you have heard of past transgressions or mistakes being referred to as "baggage." There is one thing to know about baggage. It doesn't follow you unless you are hanging onto the handle. You don't need it, so let go! People can only associate you with your baggage

if you are still hanging onto it. No one is beyond being a person of strong character, regardless of their history.

2. Focus on how you want your character perceived. Developing positive character has to be purposeful. Learn and understand how you want to see yourself and how you want others to see you. Reinforce it with practice and affirmation and expect it of yourself and others.

3. Continually fix flawed areas of your character. The reason power tests a man's character is because character is revealed by friction. It is important to prepare yourself to be a person of character, but character is not who you are entering the trials of life; rather, it is who you are emerging from the trials of life. If you didn't like who you were when you were challenged, then admit it and fix it.

Personal character is part of your journey, but it is more like the path you are walking on than the steps you are taking. Because you are unique, your path will differ from those of others, but there will be difficulties and suffering along the way. According to the Bible, in Romans, there is glory in suffering because then there is perseverance, then character, then hope. In my journey, if I hadn't seen hope in the mirror every morning, my journey would have been impossible.

Level 2 – Pursue Personal Fulfillment

Is it selfish to seek personal fulfillment? Actually, personal fulfillment has more to do with self-control than selfishness. Personal fulfillment is not the same as personal gratification. Consider this, to find personal fulfillment you might have to forego personal gratification, yet ultimately, personal fulfillment leads to personal gratification.

In your journey to personal growth you need to work on your mind, body and soul. My biggest struggle has been with my body. When I was at the height of my despair I focused heavily on mind and soul, to the neglect of my body. I have some really bad habits from stressful times where I did not pay attention to my body. There are times when I have to train my body, but I would rather work or sleep. There are times when Linda's fresh baked cookies look and smell way better than my carrot sticks. (Unfortunately, my stress activity is eating, and Linda's stress activity is baking! She doesn't eat much of her baking. She just likes to bake, so we always have baked sweets around.)

If I am going to be successful developing a healthy body, there are times I am going to have to train when I would rather sleep. There are times I'm going to have to eat carrot sticks when I would rather have the hot chocolate chip cookies I'm smelling. Paradoxically, achieving personal fulfillment requires some personal sacrifice.

It is hard to lead others if you are struggling with your own personal fulfillment. People look to their leaders to help them find theirs. Linda's business growth depends on developing a team of clients, some of whom want to build a business of their own. Case in point: when Linda enjoyed a successful career in another industry, her goal was to simply make a little extra money and earn exotic trips. When she ran across people who wanted to build a business with her, she would come home and say, for instance, "she is going to be great at this; if she works hard she could help me get to the next promotion." It was hard for Linda to help these people build a business because building a business was not part of her personal fulfillment at that time.

After years of this and not really getting a team together that stuck with the business, Linda had an epiphany which altered her view on her personal fulfillment. She came home very excited from a team meeting one evening, and said: "the more I work, the more they work, and the more I serve them, the more motivated they are." She realized that what she had to offer others was to serve them to help them find their fulfillment while she was pursuing hers.

Learn how to feel fulfillment. Have you ever reached a goal, only to become immediately unsatisfied? Have you reached a benchmark in your life and then said, "Is this it?" We tend to have an unhuman approach to objectives in the corporate world (except maybe for sales organizations). Despite the fact that humans thrive on emotions, we impersonalize success and advancement.

The corporate world tends to sell success and advancement in terms of dollars, authority, power and fame. But more often than not, we end up with disenchantment, stress, dissatisfaction and burnout—since what we really seek is fulfillment, empowerment, relationships and appreciation. The current disconnect between generations has arisen because younger generations—Millennials, for instance—overcompensated to the status quo they grew up in, shunning success and advancement when they saw the stress and burnout it caused in previous generations.

> *If your goals and objectives are entrenched in your beliefs and your emotions, then success and advancement are satisfied by your feelings and emotional fulfillment.*

In fact, the problem for previous generations wasn't success and advancement; it was what it represented. People were missing the equilibrium associated with fulfillment. If your goals and objectives are entrenched in your beliefs and your emotions, then success and advancement are *satisfied* by your feelings and emotional fulfillment. The actual goal or objective is the anchor for those feelings.

For example, if getting fit and living a healthy lifestyle makes you feel proud and excited to live life, then pride and excitement are what you are pursuing. Getting fit and living a healthy lifestyle anchors those feelings. If you start to lose your fitness and healthy lifestyle, then those feelings will fade and making progress will become a daily effort with increased stress.

In getting a promotion, you feel empowered and appreciated; the promotion anchors those feelings. If you do not continually uphold your responsibilities of that new position, then those feelings begin to recede. On the other hand, if getting a promotion makes you feel stressed and anxious, then the promotion was not the real objective. Perhaps pursuing the promotion was based more in ego than in fulfillment. The feelings are what made you fulfilled; the benchmark just anchors those feelings for you. Here is a little secret: as you pursue personal fulfillment in your personal growth you will naturally start helping others pursue fulfillment. That is part of leadership.

It's hard to consistently do your job well if you are not striving for fulfillment and leading others to do the same. There are things you can do to help stay focused on personal fulfillment. Strive to get much, but give more than you get. Strive for power, but serve more than you are served. Strive for knowledge, but teach more than you learn. Strive for authority, but give grace more than you demand submission. Strive for joy, but provide more for others than yourself. This is personal fulfillment.

Level 3 – Accumulate Personal Achievement

As you focus on personal growth there is an element that needs to be measured. There is value in having something to show for your life's efforts. Personal achievement ultimately doesn't mean much without character and fulfillment, but in concert with these, it is what highlights your growth and your leadership potential.

If you learn that the new leader of your team is a highly decorated Navy Seal who has carried out several dangerous and highly valuable missions, you will tend to have inherent respect for your new leader. If you then find out that he is disrespectful, arrogant, and lacking personal direction, then your respect is diminished. If, however, he demonstrates upstanding character and shows fulfillment in his life, then you will doubtless be a more willing member of his team.

Used in the right way, personal achievement isn't a statement of "Look at what I did!" It is a statement of "Look at what I can lead you to!" Personal achievement demonstrates planning, skills, and execution, along with some luck. You don't have to be a Navy Seal to have significant achievements. Just know what you want to achieve and work to that end. Personal achievements show you know how to be successful. The people you lead will be interested in your success because they need to know that you can lead them to success.

One last thought:

Why do you suppose it is important to emphasize mind, body, and soul in personal growth? I used this as an illustration for Personal Fulfillment, but it applies to Personal Character and Personal Achievement as well. The importance lies in completeness. Don't leave any gaps in your personal growth. How does your character apply to mind, body and soul completely? How does your fulfillment apply to mind, body, and soul completely? How do your achievements apply to mind, body, and soul completely?

Notes and Insights:

_____

_____

_____

_____

_____

_____

_____

_____

_____

_____

_____

_____

_____

_____

_____

_____

_____

_____

_____

_____

_____

_____

_____

_____

_____

_____

_____

_____

_____

CHAPTER 4:
CBA – CLARITY, BELIEF, AND ACTION

ACTION WITHOUT BELIEF IS FUTILE, belief without clarity is fragile and clarity without action is stagnant. Vision is formulated through clarity, belief, and action. To focus on Personal Character, Personal Fulfillment, and Personal Achievements, you need vision. Your vision is the bucket into which go your standards, goals, and actions, that is if you are to have meaningful personal development. Understand, though, as you grow as a person your vision may seem to change, but usually the vision is the same and it is the perspective that has changed. This shows you are evolving.

To help set and realize your vision I want to introduce a guide I use when I coach leaders. This guide, called **CBA – Clarity, Belief, and Action**, outlines a process of casting a vision and taking appropriate actions. I found CBA to be much more meaningful than the classic process of taking something you think you want and developing an action plan to get there. CBA starts with understanding your vision and why you have certain objectives and goals.

Clarity

Clarity is the understanding you need to formulate your vision. I have found it useful to say that your vision is not something you create, but a result. Pursuing clarity helps you identify your vision. If you think of the Hierarchy of Personal Development, this is where you decide what your character is going to look like, what will bring you fulfillment, and what it is you want to achieve.

When you work on "Clarity," you jump straight to what the ideal scenario looks like for you, and *then* take the time to capture how it feels to be in that ideal scenario. Imagining yourself actually *experiencing* an outcome clears the view to reveal your vision and what goals and objectives you need to realize that vision. Don't move forward too far into personal growth until you have the perspective of already having achieved your vision.

My daughter, Sarah, has a brilliant mind. As a high school student, she amazed me with her ability to think through any subject. She excelled in math and science but was not drawn to history. Thus, we were very surprised when, before her sophomore year, she enrolled in AP European History—what many students perceived to be the hardest class at her high school. Halfway through the first semester we talked about how it was going. She said she didn't enjoy studying history so intensely, **but** that she really wanted to *have* taken it and *have* earned an "A." She had the perspective of already earning an "A." She wasn't particularly enjoying her studies but wanting to do well in the most difficult class her school offered lined up with what she needed to do to get an "A." And she succeeded. It was a personal achievement goal for her. Had she spent the semester thinking about how much she didn't like history, there is a good chance she would not have met that goal.

If you have played sports, performed with a group, or been on any kind of team, then you know how important it is for everyone to contribute. Think about a team with two exceptionally talented individuals who have similar talents, but only one of whom is really successful. We may refer to the unsuccessful one as "lazy," or we may say that "Her heart isn't in it," or "He didn't have the intestinal fortitude to be successful." Equally likely is that what they *needed to do* was not aligned with what they *wanted to do* in order to succeed. They didn't have the clarity of already being successful. It was not part of their vision.

Every athlete needs to practice and condition, but how many actually like to practice and condition? Everything I read about Peyton Manning makes me think he wanted to win so much that he wanted to practice and study harder than most others. His "need to" was aligned with his "want to" in order to achieve a larger goal. Sometime, there was a five-star quarterback out of high school that never made it past his freshman year in college football because he was focused on *needing* to practice, which he dreaded. And that was more powerful than his *wanting* to be the starting quarterback. His vision was set on practice and not on being the starting quarterback.

Clarity is not easy to find, and it's even harder to help others find. Remember stereograms, those pictures with the 3D images buried in them that you stare at until the image suddenly pops out? I have seen groups of people standing in front of a display of stereograms at the mall, egging each other on to see the image. Those who find it, try to find the words to explain what others need to do to see it, and those who can't see the image contort their faces and bend their bodies in frustrated attempts. Finally, they may catch a glimpse of the image, and that's when they gain some clarity. They may eventually see the image every time they glance at the picture. That's the kind of clarity you are looking for in personal growth. It can take a while to hone in on the hidden image – but once you're aware of it, you have a much easier time catching it. People who have found clarity know who they want to be and what they need to do to succeed.

Finding clarity helps you align what you need to do with what you want to do. When you can see yourself in a place of success and it lines up with your character, fulfillment, and desired achievements, you can then start to express your vision. Once you have your vision you create your reality of living in your vision. However, until you can believe in that vision, what you need to do is not fully aligned with you want to do.

Belief

You have probably set many goals in your life and had dreams of how your life would turn out. These will just be dreams until you start to believe in your vision and yourself. It all starts with a willingness to *decide and succumb* to your belief. This starts by reflecting on the clarity that is being revealed around your personal growth and focusing on the vision you're creating for yourself. If you can start to do this now, you'll be on your way to fulfilling that vision before you even finish this book.

One thing about working with entrepreneurs is that belief is imperative to finding success, mainly because belief is often all there is. Before there are sales, a team, even a business, there is just a faith that the plan will work. In almost every call, meeting, convention, or retreat with Linda's organization, belief is emphasized—in the company, the products, the leaders, and, most importantly, in the individuals themselves.

Of course, it works the other way as well; the people who got frustrated with building a business "knew it wouldn't work" before they ever started. Or they listened to those who were not really working their business. Or sometimes they just became complacent and forgot why they started down this path in the first place. Belief is the most powerful motivator. If a person believes, they will work relentlessly for success—their own and others'. If they don't, they won't.

Sustaining belief is a significant challenge. Whether you are a start-up entrepreneur or work in an established organization, the messages around what you are doing are not always going to be positive. Some people may have had bad experiences with your organization or organizations like yours. Others don't understand what you are doing or why you would be successful doing it. There may be envy or resentment based on the success of your organization or based on your personal success or ambition.

Linda will remind her team often that action offends the inactive. People can get uncomfortable or even offended when someone in their peer group starts to put effort into personal growth. For whatever reason, you are going to confront messages that will challenge your belief: belief in your industry, belief in your organization, belief in your products, and most discerning, belief in yourself. Focus on building a belief so deep that you will be able to process negative messages in a constructive manner and even enable yourself to be propelled by these messages.

I have experience in my career with negative messages around several things I have been involved in like home builders, pharmaceutical companies, the Network Marketing industry, and even in my ability or credentials to overcome my setbacks or start my own company. I have witnessed people in Linda's organization who have built successful businesses. These people enjoy their work, have flexibility, and make more than a lot of professionals make in the corporate world. There are also thousands of people just in Linda's organization who use and appreciate the quality products. So, if someone makes disparaging claims about this industry or company, it doesn't shake my belief in the business. Our job is to instill this belief in those that have not experienced that success yet. Don't let others determine your belief! You will miss out on great opportunities.

> *Often, the evidence that validates your belief doesn't appear until you fulfill your vision.*

There are only two options here: believe or don't believe. If you are going to pursue a vision, choose to believe. Often, the evidence that validates your belief doesn't appear until you fulfill your vision. Choose to continue to believe even if the "how" is unclear. Choose to surround yourself with messages and people that remind you of why you believe.

In my corporate experience, I have seen plenty of leaders spending minimal time and effort in building belief. Imagine a corporate organization that depended on employees' belief to inspire success. What if the difference between success and failure was based on each employee's belief? How would you lead differently?

Most individuals who work in highly structured organizations do their job adequately without belief or purpose at all. They work simply because it is their job—and many are compensated whether they do their job *well* or not. Leaders in these types of companies have little power to shape the long-term culture. If leaders in a corporate setting instilled a strong belief in the work their teams are doing, imagine how that would impact the culture.

Tie in Emotion with Belief

Linda's compensation plan includes promotions based on sales volume. When working with people in Linda's organization who are trying to get one of these promotions, we discuss their belief and their "why" as well as "how." But what is interesting is that when they initially start talking about promotions they tend to speak in vague terms and are rather matter of fact—like they are making a list: make extra money, time flexibility, etc.

Then, when I listen to the leaders on Linda's team who have achieved these promotions talk about their "why," I notice they usually couch it as an emotion. For instance, what extra money means to their family and how time flexibility helps them serve a family member in need. When they really believe in their "why," it becomes a feeling—and then they tend to be more successful. Usually there are tears involved because of how important this "why" that propelled them to success is to them. They are already starting to feel the belief; we just try to get them to internalize it, so they feel the emotion of their success.

As you reflect on your own vision for personal growth, think about what is so important about your "why" that makes you emotional to think about it? Was it proving something to yourself or someone else? Was it that you can do things now that are important to you that you never could before? Did you heal or fortify an important relationship in your life by reaching this objective?

How do you internalize your objectives that are consistent with your clarity? *What makes an objective so important that you don't feel right if you don't do something every day to accomplish it?* If you are trying to be a better networker, maybe it fulfills a purpose to be a more meaningful part of more people's lives. In getting a degree, you feel personal pride and increased confidence in pursuing opportunities.

Maybe getting fit allows you to enjoy your life more and be more confident around people. *Learn to feel your vision, to fulfill your dream.*

After Super Bowl 50, Cam Newton, the quarterback for the losing Carolina Panthers, was intolerable and walked out in the middle of the post-game press conference. After he walked out, the media piled on. "Cam was a sore loser." "He acted unsportsmanlike." When someone in the media asked him later why he acted that way he said, "… I have a mentality, I have a standard I set for myself …," my sense was that he believed and felt so strongly that his team was going to win that it was inconceivable to him that they didn't. He didn't know how to act because it was counter to what had become fact to him. I find his actions fascinating. This is a case study in belief and feeling your objectives. Can you build that kind of belief in your company, your job and yourself—the kind where failure is simply *inconceivable*?

I am not a Steve Jobs historian, but from what I have read about him, he wasn't set on building the most profitable computer company in the world. He was passionate about building the most innovative and practical products for the consumer, products that would change people's lives. He was more satisfied with a project that transformed people's lives than its initial marketability or profitability.

This is what made Jobs a marketer's nightmare; it is difficult to do market research on products that fix a problem people don't even know they have yet. He could be hard to work with because the products met his approval when they "felt right," and not necessarily if they met engineering specifications, marketing specifications, or budgets.

If you find the emotions of why you have a certain objective, you can really start to discuss belief. More times than not, lack of success does not have to do with lack of knowledge, skill, or experience. Granted, all three can get you a long way in your career and in life, but they do not assure long-term success. Rather, success is determined by how much you believe in something—how much you understand *why* you're aiming for a certain goal. For every talented singer with a successful music career, there are thousands of equally talented singers who never made their music career work. For every successful vice president or even CEO, there are thousands of highly competent managers who don't move up in their company because they don't truly see themselves in those positions. Don't say you believe until you are emotionally invested in what you are trying to accomplish. At this point your vision is becoming undeniable.

Action

A New Year's resolution is usually something that would be desirable if it happened, but, it is hard to take action on unless it is part of your vision. CBA (Clarity, Belief, Action) teaches you the concepts you'll in turn teach your team in their own personal growth journey. You'll start to see growth through **constantly** revealing your clarity and deciding to believe, but you won't see results until you act. This is where you will accumulate Personal Achievements.

I mentioned earlier that vision is the bucket your goals, objectives and actions go in. The reason you develop clarity and belief first is to give teeth to your action plans to meet your goals and objectives for your vision. The goal is to get to the point where it takes more energy to *not* follow through with your plans than it does to complete them. Most of us have had times that we know what to do but can't seem to get it done. We can sometimes get in a mad loop where we plan and prepare, know what to do, but then don't do it. So, we plan and prepare again, know what to do … and then don't do it again. We keep going through the cycle, thinking things will be different each time. It might click eventually, but it's not simply because you went through the cycle several times—it's because you found clarity and belief in what you wanted.

I advocate taking advantage of coaching, planning, and training whenever you can. No matter what level of leader you become, everyone needs guidance along the way. Lack of action isn't an issue with training, though; it's that you need to find clarity and belief to encourage action.

I want the leaders I coach to experience personal growth, so they know what it feels like to lead a team through the process. I often envision I am working with someone who has always wanted to skydive and is preparing to do so for the first time. You can talk about and simulate skydiving all day long, but when someone looks out an open door at 13,000 feet above earth, everything becomes very real. This is not a time to decide if you want to skydive or not; this is a time for action. Clarity means that they have the desire to make it from here to there safely. Belief is folded up and strapped on their back waiting to deploy when needed. And, finally, Action is taking that first step from the solid floor of the plane to nothing but air.

Notice in this illustration that Belief isn't a safety net you can see down below. It is a culmination of preparation, competence, confidence and trust. You have to decide to believe your parachute is viable before you jump. You have to realize that belief isn't validated until you take action. Don't be the person that deploys the parachute on the plane just to make sure it works okay. That's not belief. *Belief always manifests itself after you have started the freefall* (that's why you have to decide to believe). Many great plans, innovated initiatives, creative projects, and thus personal growth never come to be because people didn't take that first step.

When we talked about clarity, we discussed the process where you projected yourself in a position where you have already achieved your goal, so you know what it feels like. The action plan is similar in that you want to align your plan as close to clarity as possible. Clarity and Belief help you align what you *need to do* with what you *want to do*. You are working backwards from when you imagined your success and focused on the feelings and emotions of that success to where you take action. *The goal here is to create a process, like the skydiver—to generate momentum so great that it would be very difficult to fail.*

One sign that you are taking significant action in personal growth is that you are overwhelmed with anticipation from personal action. Do you live in a constant state of anticipation? If not, you need to evaluate the actions you are taking. Anticipation serves as a "steroid" of sorts for action. For personal growth, it can be the difference between success and status quo. Read through this list and think about the feeling you had while you waited for a reaction or feedback when you...

- Wrote to a special someone how you felt about them

- Filled out a college application

- Took an important test you studied hard for

- Interviewed for a job or a promotion

- Filled out a loan application for a new home

- Made a proposal to an important client or committee

- Asked for a raise

- Applied for a grant for an important research project

- Made a significant presentation, performance, or audition

Every action might not have an immediate result, but every action immediately *anticipates* a result. I like to say that not every action has instant *gratification*, but every action always has instant anticipation. For example, if you work out or go on a diet you might not see changes for every action you take or decision you make. In fact, that is why so many people struggle with sticking to a healthy lifestyle—because they don't see results right away. But if you can convince yourself after every action you take or good decision you make that you can anticipate a transformation someday, you will be more likely to stick to your plan. If you can master this and apply it to your personal growth you will be motivated to act every day.

In 2005, my family went to visit my cousin and her family in London. While there, we planned a vacation to the island of Tenerife, one of the Canary Islands off the west coast of Africa. It is a beautiful island, and the beach we stayed near was composed of black sand created by basalt deposits left from rapidly cooling lava many years ago. It was intriguing thinking about lava pouring over the very beaches we were playing on.

While there, we learned a bit of the history. The neighboring island of La Palma has an ominous story. The volcano on La Palma has a side that has bulged from pressure from the rising magma that scientists believe makes this volcano structurally unstable. Another eruption could create a landslide so powerful that it might trigger a major tsunami that could hit the East Coast of the United States within eight hours. Even though the likelihood of this event is disputed, if I hear of an eruption of a volcano in the Canary Islands, my family and I will be avoiding the East Coast for a day or so. The intriguing thing is that if it were ever to occur, observing the Atlantic Ocean in between, you would barely see the energy billowing towards the United States coast.

Why not? The mountain collapsing on La Palma pushes down into the ocean with so much force that it creates a massive stream of energy that builds as it travels *through* the Atlantic. At this point, no one above can see significant signs of anything happening. Then, as all this energy starts to approach the shallow shores of the East Coast, it starts to suck in water off the shore line. As the sea recedes, the water is forced upwards until it creates a gigantic wall roaring towards land. Imagine standing on the Jersey shore and you suddenly see the surf receding drastically back into the ocean. Then you see a 20-foot wall of water coming towards you!

People who take significant actions create energy that moves unnoticed until it has nowhere else to go and creates an overwhelming result. People who take consistent and significant action cause consistent movement of energy that we call momentum. Similar to the tsunami, action was taken, and energy is building through a series of events that might go unnoticed. Some people get discouraged when they don't see immediate results from their actions, but if you stay in action you are building momentum.

There is a word the world tends to use for people who are in this state of momentum: *lucky*. Of course, it's not luck at all; it just seems like it. Two people might take the same action, but one is actively anticipating an effect and stays in action, while the other is not. When opportunity arrives for the person who anticipated an effect, they are ready to take action on the opportunity because they stayed in momentum. The second person is oblivious and unprepared for the opportunity and tends to react to the person anticipating the effect by saying: "They're always so lucky!"

An example may be when you pursue a promotion before there is an opening, you might research the prerequisites for that promotion, fulfill those prerequisites and make sure the powers that be are aware of your efforts. Then, when the position opens up you aren't surprised if you are the top candidate for the job. If you continue to do your job well and network to learn of other desirable positions, you might find yourself with multiple or successive promotion opportunities. All the while, others are wondering why you are so lucky.

The key is to be consistent in your actions and never minimize the value of anything you do, no matter how seemingly small. When I started as a representative with Merck, I was pretty ignorant—of the products, the industry, the company, and the medical field overall. I demonstrated my ignorance almost daily. But I purposefully put effort into learning everything I could about my job, especially the market I was responsible for. I created binders of information to help me understand how our products moved and who moved them.

At times, I felt like I was doing a lot of busy work that had little value because it was neither required nor expected. But this was an important analysis for me, personally, to help me understand my book of business. Within a few months of working in my territory, the company launched a new initiative. Immediately, I knew my analysis would benefit this initiative. All the while, I had developed a better understanding of our products and built relationships with my customers. A couple of months later, my territory was out-performing all the other territories in the district and, as I found out later, performing best in the nation.

I had no way of knowing all the ways my activities were going to benefit me when I was completing them; I was simply trying to understand my role better. Yet, I was always looking for opportunities based on my actions because I was anticipating them. From this point on, if I felt any action had any potential, I worked on it. Sometimes it was years before I realized its value, but I always anticipated that my actions were going to have future value.

A leader consistently uses anticipation to drive activity for themselves and for their teams. You can anticipate an effect from today's activity, and a more significant effect if you do the same thing tomorrow. The effect grows exponentially the more consecutive days you complete that activity. The longer this goes on, the more you are surrounded by opportunities. Soon, the majority of your activities are focused on capitalizing on opportunities. Keep your team anticipating great things from their actions, and opportunities for great things will become the standard.

Anyone *can be* a leader; everyone *should be* a leader. Consciously begin to look in the mirror in the morning and see a leader staring back. Continually engage in personal growth. Understand your Clarity, Belief, and Actions. Anticipate the opportunities that your activities present to you. Push the limits to succeed, and coach your team to do the same. Anticipate great things, and your team will anticipate great things.

One last thought:
Action is not easy. Action requires effort and causes friction. It is easier to settle for the status quo. However, if you have a clear vision of where you need to be and a strong belief in your vision and yourself, the status quo starts to become uncomfortable. What is it that you know you need to be pursuing but you suppress because you know it is something you are going to have to work for?

Notes and Insights:

_____
_____
_____
_____
_____
_____
_____
_____
_____
_____
_____
_____
_____
_____
_____
_____
_____
_____
_____
_____
_____
_____
_____
_____
_____
_____
_____

Chapter 5:
Sticky Note Training

I WANT TO TAKE YOU through an exercise I developed to help groups get out of a rut or when they hit a lull in accomplishing their objectives towards their vision. Usually I am working with a group that has common goals and the group feeds off each other's energy. But I will modify it here to illustrate using CBA for personal development. I call this the Sticky Note Exercise because we use three large sticky note sheets and put them on the wall in front of the group.

Sticky Note Exercise Step 1

What objective for personal growth do you have that is part of your vision—something you have not done yet but want to? Think about this for a minute, and then write the objective down. It could be getting a degree, getting in shape, serving others, getting a promotion, acquiring a specific skill, or changing your attitude. You could think broader and bigger: embracing a life-changing opportunity, being atop your selected industry/sport or launching a business. Next, imagine that you have written your objective on a poster-size sticky note at the top of a page.

Now, prepare to close your eyes and clear your mind. We are going to simulate sleep, or rather, waking up. When you wake up in the morning there is always that moment that you have to recollect your thoughts and realize what day it is, what you have to do today, and, if you travel a lot, even where you are. This is the effect you want when you open your eyes. To make this work you have to insert a "reality" that you are going to realize when you open your eyes and reorient yourself. The "reality" I want you to insert is that you have already achieved the objective that you wrote down. Now close your eyes for about 5 minutes and think about that reality, then open your eyes.

Good Morning! Congratulations on achieving your objective! It is important that you know what it *feels* like to reach this objective. I want you to describe how it feels now that you have reached that objective. Read through the following questions and describe on the lines provided or a piece of paper how it feels to find success from the perspective of having accomplished your objective. Find someone special to you, share this with them, and discuss it.

- What have I proven to myself?

  _____

  _____

  _____

- What does my day look like? How is it different now?

  _____

  _____

  _____

- What am I able to do now that I could not do before?

  _____

  _____

  _____

- What does my spouse or special someone say about me to others?

_____

_____

_____

- What is my spouse or special someone saying to me? What about my kids, parents, or other family members?

_____

_____

_____

- How am I better able to invest in the passions of those close to me?

_____

_____

_____

- Do I feel a sense of joy, pride, relief, or satisfaction in reaching this objective?

_____

_____

_____

- How am I able to better contribute to my family, business, community, or charity?

_____

_____

_____

- What new opportunities are open to me now?

_____

_____

Keep your notes handy—you will refer to them in a moment.

Sticky Note #1 Example

How are things different? What does it feel like?
Objective: Completed my MBA
- I have proven to myself I can set an objective and accomplish it
- I am satisfied that effort has more value than complacency
- I am proud because my spouse brags on me to our friends how smart I am and how hard I worked even though there were times it was hard on them.
- My parents keep telling me how proud they are of me
- It feels really good to write "MBA" on my email signature
- I am more confident because I feel like I have more to offer with my credentials and expanded education.
More examples of Notes at www.teakleader.com

Clarity and Belief Bring Momentum

When I work with Linda as she develops people in her business, we focus on a system with a proven track record. When Linda trains and teaches the system, most people understand it and want to work according to it. However, when people haven't been able to meet their goals months or years in, they will ask her: "What do I need to do to make this work?" We know—*they* likely also know—*what* to do. What they are really asking is, "why can't I make myself do what needs to be done to make this work?" They know the system works; they just need to believe it will work for them.

They are usually holding onto some other belief that is limiting their success. Once you've imagined reaching your projected objective and have looked at how it's affected your life, think back on what you might have been clinging to that prevented you from believing in yourself and achieving this goal. Your belief was in something, just not what you need to be successful. For instance, I struggle to consistently work to stay fit. Sometimes I believe strongly in the value of healthy eating and exercise and I tend to do it. Other times I have a stronger belief that I deserve or earned the right to drink soda, eat dessert, or not work out. I still believe in healthy living; I just have a stronger belief that I deserve to eat poorly or rest at times.

I was recently talking to the son of some close friends at a high school football game. Jake has graduated now but played linebacker for this same high school a couple of years ago, and we were watching his younger brother Zeke play his same position. We were discussing a situation where the defense got pinned against their end zone. The other team had first down on the 5-yard line with goal to go.

Jake told me that he loved playing in those situations, because regardless of what had happened in the game to that point, it was very clear what the objective was right at that moment. He said he always felt like he and his teammates were going to stop the other team. All energy was focused on each down, and each time they stopped the opponent, their belief that they could continue to do so got stronger. This belief reduces distractions (which helps you focus on action).

The key is to grow momentum to a point that your belief and clarity are building on each other. This helps eliminate the distractions. If you're having trouble gaining momentum, focus on a piece of your story you're trying to develop at this time. What is the **next** step you need to take to be successful? Build your belief in just that **next** step, even if it's only a small one. You are that defense backed up against the goal line. Don't look at the grand scheme; look at the next thing to be done. Then move to the next moment until you've enjoyed a series of wins which gives you more clarity upon which to build your belief.

There is more energy and excitement with each down the football team prevents the other team from scoring. Again, look back on something you've done well in the past and ask yourself: what was the moment in that story where I really built my momentum? Can

49

you capture that clarity and belief again, and use it to reach your next objective?

Other distractions to belief might be just managing the sheer demands of your life. I hear a common story in Linda's organization that's a variation on this theme: her people wanted to be able to provide more for their family than they could in their current situation. It was a struggle for them because becoming successful in almost anything consumes time, and that usually means time away from family. How could a venture that takes time from your family help you provide more for your family? However, as these individuals grew their business, they realized how much more flexible their time was and how much more quality of life they could provide for their families. Basically, how much more fulfilled they were. The positive reaction from their families only strengthened their belief.

> **Balance is where everything important to you has a time when it takes a priority.**
> **- Joel Parker**

You need to find enough clarity and belief to take that first step and get your momentum going. But this means understanding what your priority at that season in your life is. I certainly believe in balance in our lives but what that means to me is *everything that is important to you has a time when it takes a priority for a period of time.* If a mom is going back to school to get her MBA she might not be available to make dinner and attend activities during finals week. Others will have to fill that role for her during that week, so she can focus on doing well in her courses.

The definition applies even if you are trying to find balance on a daily basis. A dad who usually takes his children to school in the mornings might have to make other arrangements if he has a critical early meeting one morning. But that evening he might forgo a business dinner to make it to his child's vocal concert. Although this example spans just a day, such balance is typically achieved through a series of moments which may be days, weeks, or years.

Priority doesn't have to mean exclusivity, either. The mom getting her MBA might not be able to do her typical routine, but she can take moments to engage with her family during finals week. When Jake and Zeke focused on that moment to stop the offense from scoring, it didn't mean they ignored the fundamentals of the game plan. When you are thinking about balance and are focused on the priority of that moment it doesn't mean you ignore the fundamentals of your life. It just means that these other things are managed while you focus on your current priority. Understand what your priority is at this moment, and eliminate the distractions going on around you. Focus on your belief in this priority.

Let's return to the objective that you imagined you achieved. Once you've achieved it, people are going to ask how you got there. Reflect on the list you made of how it feels to have accomplished the objective. Looking back, it all seems so simple (and maybe even destined), but you know there were challenges and struggles. Some of those challenges might have had you questioning your ability, fortitude, or even worthiness to achieve your goal. But that seems like silliness now that you've gotten to where you want to be.

Look back as well on the skills and abilities you used in previous successes in your life. These are the same skills that can make you successful now. When you need to build belief, it's critical to not allow yourself to look around and get distracted. Don't think that others' visions are more important than yours. Don't let how fast or slow others are reaching their goals take your mind off your own. Don't be distracted if they are using different skills and abilities to reach their goal. In reaching your objective, think about how you had exactly what it took to pursue the objective and stay focused on that.

We talked earlier about feeling that objective instead of just stating it. Now you are pursuing that feeling. Again, focus on the feeling you have when you imagine yourself achieving that objective. Learn to incite that feeling when you're on your actual journey. Understand that this objective may be a major transformation in your life, or simply a daily task. Whichever it is, *anticipating that feeling is the journey and reaching that feeling is the achievement*. The objective or task is the means to that feeling.

Sticky Note Exercise Step 2

Now we progress from Sticky Note #1 to Sticky Note #2. Remember, your reality is you have already accomplished this objective. Write down what your objective was and a short statement about your Clarity and Belief at the top. Here you imagine a list of the actions you took. **Write that list down.** How do these action items tie into your Clarity and Belief? **Write that down.** At this point you are not so worried about the order of events, just the actions you took to achieve success. Remember, you have already been there in your mind.

> *Think of it like this, Clarity fills Belief and Belief fuels Action.*

Typically, when you sit down with the boss (or yourselves) and hatch an action plan you start with where you are now and create steps up through your plan, like climbing a mountain. The CBA Action Plan is different because it builds its own momentum. With CBA you have already envisioned yourself succeeding in the plan, so it is like you have started at the top and mapped out every ledge and foothold you need to use on your way up. This way you have more confidence and excitement going up the mountain.

Your ownership and enthusiasm for the action plan increase the more they are tied to your Clarity and Belief. The action is in the order of attack (bottom of the mountain), but the planning starts at clarity (top of the mountain). Focus on the action closest to clarity first, then the previous action and so on. Do you feel more ownership of the action plan as you move through it? Do you feel more enthusiasm for getting to the next action steps? Are you anticipating the next step in the process? Think of it like this, Clarity fills Belief and Belief fuels Action.

The CBA process recognizes that personal growth must be purposeful. Look back at some defining moments of personal growth in your life; odds are, there was a moment of clarity, even if an unwelcome event forced it upon you. In my case, when I was down, broke, and out of options, I had to make a purposeful decision to find the courage to understand there would be opportunities when there didn't seem to be any. This helped me grow as a leader who forges ahead for myself and my team to discover opportunities.

I couldn't have maintained that courage if I hadn't had belief and hope that with God's help I would be in a better situation. In fact, I had no room for anything but certainty that I was going to succeed. Finally, my actions were tied to a feeling and desire that went deeper than just knowing what to do. Implementing CBA is a purposeful way to accomplish what you need to accomplish in personal growth.

Read over your list and think about the reasons why you're doing these Action items. Are they consistent with your Clarity and Belief? Do you feel the importance of that action when you read each item? Do you feel emotionally tied to that action?

Now, on the sticky note, go through the list and mark each item chronologically, start numbering closest to clarity of success (last action item). You will put a "1" closest to achieving success; look at the action that is happening closest to accomplishing the objective, then ask: what happens *before* this? Put a "2" next to that action. This will help you visualize how each item supports your Clarity and Belief and will give you momentum.

Now look at the **first action** you need to take. This will be the **highest number**, so you are counting down to your objective. How compelled do you feel to do the first item, right now? Focus on the comments you made about *why* you need to do this—and not so much what the item is. This should incite a sense of eagerness to get started and move through the list with Clarity and Belief getting stronger as you go. You should feel you *want* to take these actions as much as you *need* to take these actions.

Sticky Note #2

How did I do it?
Objective: Completed my MBA; Clarity and Belief: I will be an executive one day where I can influence organizational culture. An MBA gives me confidence in my credentials, abilities, and knowledge. I demonstrated to myself, my family and business associates my focus and determination to better myself.
7 - I made a decision I was going to do it (I am determined I can accomplish anything I put effort in to).
6 - I got organized and researched the right program for me and did what it took to be accepted (The skills I implement now will help me be successful).
5 - I made it a priority and put all my energy into it even when others were skeptical (I am in charge of my own life).
1 - I never quit doing the required work. Often didn't feel like doing "homework" but stayed on it when I needed to (The energy I put into every detail will help me be successful)
4 - I got engaged with the other students and we relied on each other for encouragement and information (I am determined not to close myself off to benefit from new relationships and friendships)
3 - There were times I had to step out of my comfort zone to complete group projects or research (I can be bold and determined)
2 - I asked for help and support when I needed it (I was focused on the goal and used all available resources to accomplish it)
More examples of Notes at www.teakleader.com

Sticky Note Exercise Step 3

The third and final "sticky note" is to eliminate the distractions in action. As we discussed, starting with clarity and belief does a lot of this work; however, we still need to be prepared for new distractions. Issues like unsupportive family or close friends, ambiguous or artificial deadlines, aggressive dissenters of your plan, personal weaknesses, or destructive tendencies can all keep you from reaching goals. A critical step is to create triggers to identify these distractions, and counter-measures to confront them.

Sticky Note #3

What distractions did I mitigate?
Objective: Completed my MBA
- Husband, family, and friends may not understand my commitment and limited availability. They may pressure me to do something instead of what I needed to do for school <u>Triggers</u> – Guilt, Phrases like "you're too busy for us", FOMO: Fear Of Missing Out. <u>Countermeasures</u> – Remember your feelings when friends and family were proud of your accomplishments.
- Work and school is exhausting, and my schedule is unpredictable. Everything seems top priority. <u>Triggers</u> – You start getting overwhelmed with amount of work to do. You will get tired, that is part of it. <u>Countermeasures</u> – Remember satisfaction of completing the program.
- There are others that are smarter or have more experience in the program. <u>Triggers</u> – Doubt or loss of confidence. Despair when you have set backs with bad grade or evaluation. <u>Countermeasures</u> – Remember the pride when your husband and kids brag how smart you are.
More examples of Notes at www.teakleader.com

When my son, Preston, ran cross-country, I noticed some correlation between how runners train, and this sticky note training. When kids first start in cross-country, their tendency is to sprint out of the start—then as they tire, they realize everyone is passing them. Many end up walking because they can't maintain the pace. Running a long distance is hard, it hurts, and there are a lot of better runners.

Most novice runners thought it was going to be easier. This is typically how we approach an action plan.

As the season goes on, the coach tries to identify an ending time for each athlete as a target. They learn how to pace themselves, and parents or coaches are often yelling out times to their kids, so they know where they are at certain distances. However, every once in a while, a kid gets distracted by others passing them and they abandon their plan. At that point, they find themselves performing worse because they didn't manage their energy. The trained athlete judges his own body, knowing when he can push a little harder to improve his time. But he also stays disciplined, because he knows where he wants to end up and what his body can do.

The untrained cross-country runner usually wants to stop running and start walking. The trained athlete keeps running. Both are tired and uncomfortable during the race; but the trained athlete is more likely to find success because he wants to push instead of quitting. The untrained runner needs to run, which is painful and difficult, but *wants* to walk. The trained runner *needs* to beat his time or win, which is rewarding and fulfilling, so he *wants* to run. See the difference? What one *needs* to do is what the other *wants* to do.

By training with the end in mind and understanding his body, the trained athlete has already eliminated some distractions. He's not worrying about what other runners are doing or the pain and exhaustion. He also remains aware of potential distractions like trail conditions, weather, or hydration needs and will plan accordingly to minimize those distractions. While others might use those potential distractions as an excuse, the trained athlete is anticipating the distractions and has a plan to find success despite them.

Imagine yourself having imagined success, and you are approaching your limits. At this point, you're likely more focused on how to push past those limits than yielding to them. Instead of just agreeing that your action plan is reasonable to accomplish your goals, you're likely eager to *exceed* what that plan requires, because you've already experienced that feeling of success.

Think about the daily tasks you are required to do. Do you dread them? Drudge through them? Ignore them? Understand why you do these tasks, why they are a benefit to the organization or yourself and determine what you can learn from these activities. Discover what opportunities are ahead because of your experience with these tasks or the results from completing them. Realize—perhaps even appreciate— how they line up with and support your goals and ambitions.

Work hard on finding Clarity in your personal character, personal fulfillment and personal achievements through developing your story. Build a robust Belief in yourself and your goals and align your Actions with this clarity and belief. Be aware of the distractions and make plans to overcome them. Then you can begin to imagine leading yourself and a team that is always pushing its limits to succeed—a team focused on excellence.

What might you accomplish with such a team?

One last thought:

It is powerful to believe in a feeling over an objective. This is because a feeling cannot be contrived. It just feels right. Take an objective or even a vision and contemplate it for a moment. Maybe try this with alternative objectives or visions. Which one conjures the strongest feelings of fulfillment. Consider why. Use the sticky notes to work through these feelings.

Notes and Insights:

_____

_____

_____

_____

_____

_____

_____

_____

_____

_____

_____

_____

_____

_____

_____

_____

_____

_____

_____

_____

_____

_____

_____

_____

_____

_____

_____

_____

CHAPTER 6:
YOUR STORY – IT'S WHAT YOU MAKE IT!

ONE OF THE JOYS OF my position with my consulting business and partnering with Linda is being involved in so many success stories. That is a valuable lesson for leaders: EVERYBODY has a story and collectively they form a beautiful mosaic. As you develop your story it is appropriate for the leader in you to start to ask: *what am I doing to help make other people's stories success stories?*

Your story is the culmination of your continuing personal development. Why is character important to you? What fulfills you? What have you achieved? Dig deeper and understand with clarity where you want to be and what it feels like to be there. Why do you believe in what you are doing and the actions you are taking to get there? Developing a story is something I challenge leaders who work in corporate organizations or small businesses to implement because it helps their team relate to them.

A key element to anyone's story is honesty. This must be the real you. Your story must be authentic. The objective for your story is growth, not show. When you're trying to figure out where you want your story to lead you, you have to be honest and vulnerable. You might not yet be the person you're aiming to be. But you will eventually need to tell your complete story—with all your mistakes and imperfections—for it to have a significant impact on others. You need to understand where you were, where you are, and where you want to be as you focus on personal character, personal fulfillment, and personal achievement.

The stories people really want to hear—those they find most compelling—are those that demonstrate triumph, success, or healing. We are often intrigued with stories of decline, tragedy, or sorrow, but these are usually cautionary tales. Another story to avoid is a story of apathy, when you are just spinning your wheels. As you prepare your story, think about what makes it fascinating; and if it isn't, do something about it. Most strong leaders took a risk, showed persistence, had fortitude, or demanded excellence of themselves at some point in their journey. If you are alive, you are still developing your story. Make it a good one.

A clear, compelling story is what makes leaders so powerful. When we understand how someone came to a leadership position, we make a positive emotional connection with them. Most team members know they're "supposed to" follow their leader because they're a manager or an executive; but in challenging times a team needs to also know *who* they are following. Stories let those who would follow you know what you've been through, and why you are who you are. When you

> *When we understand how someone came to a leadership position, we make a positive emotional connection with them.*

communicate your story, focus on telling how you built personal character, found personal fulfillment, and accomplished personal achievements.

The Rest of My Story

I've told some of my story at the very beginning of the book. I mentioned during the first chapter that I spent the early part of my career getting my "Ph.D. in Life and Leadership." I had an expensive education: I had to spend money and mental capacity on fixing mistakes instead of on degrees. I felt good about myself and my career until I faced adversity that I wasn't prepared for—adversity that only experience can prepare you for. In this way, I needed failures. I needed that traumatic experience to change the very core of me. It was a "business boot camp" of sorts.

Soon after my low point during those times in the car, Linda and I contemplated a strategy to rise out of our financial devastation. We knew that bankruptcy was something we wanted to avoid. We had faith in the gifts God gave us that we could work ourselves out of this turmoil. This was a moment for me to challenge my personal character.

With Linda at home and a new baby on the way, I needed to start working on my new career, and soon. Before I got my degree in Construction Science at the University of Oklahoma, I pursued a degree in Chemistry at York College in York, Nebraska. I loved science and realized I had a knack for sales and marketing with my design and building business. I recognized a path to personal fulfillment. After researching career options, I sought a career in medical sales. At the time, in 1997, it was a robust, competitive field.

Landing that position was a long and arduous process. I had no real experience in that field, and very little money to live on. In December 1997 I noticed an ad in the paper (what we did before the Internet) for job interviews with Merck Pharmaceuticals in Dallas. Interviews started at 8:00 a.m. the next day. Dallas was about three and half hours from our home in Edmond, Oklahoma. With no money for a hotel, I decided to drive at 4:00 a.m. the next morning.

I hadn't understood from the ad that this was a job fair for *several* companies. When I got to the designated hotel at 7:30 a.m., there was already a long line to get in. I eventually checked in and spent part of the day interviewing. After a few interviews I finally sat down with Chris, the Manager with Merck. We were both about the same age with young families, and that helped break the ice as we discussed being young fathers.

When I told him I had my own business designing and building homes, he replied that he was currently having a home built. We discussed materials and design. He said his brother was in construction and he understood the business well. This helped because I could relate my experience to the questions he was asking without too much explanation. Again, I remember thinking that God had to have blessed me with this opportunity. As I left, he gave a very strong indication that he would be recommending me for a second interview the following month in San Antonio.

I drove home excited, but tired. It was evening now, and I had to stop halfway home for a nap. It was frigid out, but I had to shut off the car because I couldn't afford to waste gas. I also couldn't call home because we couldn't afford cell phones or a long-distance call. When I arrived home at 10:00 p.m. I was greeted with that concerned, frustrated and anxious reaction that one would expect from a wife who was home all day with a new baby and hadn't heard from her husband. Especially when all she could do is wait to hear about the prospects of this potentially life-altering opportunity. Linda was more apt to make things happen, not wait around.

By Christmas I was growing anxious that I wasn't going to hear from Chris again. Two more weeks passed. Chris had already run out of business cards when we met in Dallas, so I had no way to contact him. He had simply given me his name and said to "look me up" if I didn't hear from him. He had *seemed* genuinely interested and had even prepped me for how to handle the next round of interviews. I decided I was going to pursue this lead unless someone insisted I stop calling.

Initially, I had no luck tracking him down because I was not even sure what city he lived in. In desperation, I looked up the first phone listing for Merck I could find and called, asking for Chris. In a company of over 50,000 employees, that was a huge crap-shoot—and it didn't pay off. My next move was to call Merck's Dallas regional office. The person I reached didn't know Chris but sent me to a random voicemail. I learned later that Chris worked out of the regional office in Phoenix. But I didn't know it at the time, so I called a different division of Merck and left *another* random voicemail.

By the second week of January I had almost lost all hope. Then I got a phone call.

"Hi, this is Chris with Merck. We met in Dallas in December, and I understand you are trying to get ahold of me."

I got the deflating sense that he didn't remember me at first, which may have been, but at least we were talking now. He wanted to fly me down for interviews in San Antonio. He told me he had a family emergency the day we met in Dallas and had to leave the job fair abruptly soon after we talked. He left all his afternoon interview notes and resumes and was never able to recover them. If I hadn't reached out, he never would have called me.

Within a week, I was in San Antonio dressed to the nines, briefcase in hand. I met with Chris, then with his boss and another manager. Then it was back to the airport. After that whirlwind day, I found myself anxiously waiting again. Mercifully, it wasn't as long a wait. Chris called to offer me the job, but it wasn't finalized yet. Fortunately, I had told Chris about our financial struggles, because my background check revealed our debt. Chris said he had fought for me, but we needed to wait for an all-clear. It wasn't for another week that I was approved—just days before I was to report to training.

This experience prepared me to conquer challenges more than post-graduate degrees or an easier career path would have done. This "PhD" phase of my life was extremely valuable. Once I got the job at Merck, Linda and I were able to dissolve practically all our business debt. I earned four promotions in six years. I was enjoying my job and even felt grateful for the difficulty I endured getting it, since those experiences changed who I was as a business person. Working through the hardship made me a better person. It was a series of great personal achievements for me.

In the decade since resigning from Merck to start my consulting business, we have attained a new level of success. We are generating a personal income several times more than what I made at Merck. Several leaders in Linda's organization are high-income earners and many others are not far behind. From here, I have Clarity in my goal to leverage our successes. By serving others, we help them develop into strong, successful leaders.

Understand Your Experiences

It's critical to identify and fully live those experiences that impact your life and appreciate how they transform and improve you. This may mean taking risks and blasting outside of your comfort zone. Once you overcome difficulties and are able to move past taxing circumstances, you are better off for having that experience, regardless of the outcome.

We tend to judge failure by the results, but every failure has clues to success.

Of course, it doesn't always feel this way when you're in the middle of such situations. Sometimes when you are beat up, you want to cave in. And, you will hear from yourself, and others, plenty of good reasons to cave in. Don't give in to this temptation! Nothing is more inspiring than people who get back up after everyone—including themselves—thought they were down. It is hard to realize this because your story may not hinge on a single significant event, but an accumulation of smaller peaks and valleys that got you to the place you are now. Be aware of those and their accumulated effect on you—specifically, whether they've distracted you from your goals or helped you achieve them. Embrace "failures." We tend to judge failure by the results, but every failure has clues to success. Know that every experience in your life has lessons for future success.

I remember an instance when I had attended one of my son's eighth grade basketball games. Preston is not driven towards organized sports, but he is athletic and enjoyed playing basketball. He improved a lot in eighth grade but didn't have a strong ambition to continue to play after that year. During this game, however, he was on fire—scoring several points, rebounding, and blocking several shots. It was a close game. With less than a minute left, Preston scored to put his team up by one. In this game, Preston was the superstar.

On the other team's long pass down court, Preston's teammate stole the ball and threw towards Preston, who was still down court near the sideline. The clock was winding down and the opposing team hurried back to defend as Preston lunged to catch the pass. Preston's momentum in his motion to catch the ball was driving him out of bounds. In the heat of the moment, Preston decided to shoot and try for a basket instead of turning the ball over out of bounds. The ball bounced off the rim into a defender's hands—who then dribbled down the court to score the winning basket at the buzzer.

Of course, some of Preston's teammates were upset—but most encouraged him. I didn't want him to feel discouraged; he'd played a great game.

"Hey Buddy, I'm proud of you." I told him. "I'm proud you had the confidence to take that last shot. That's the way champions think. They always think they can make it."

"I wish I had made it," he responded. "but I bet the kid who made the last basket was happy. That was exciting for him. I'm happy for him."

That is actually the way Preston thinks. I didn't tell him I wasn't as gracious.

I wanted to make sure he was okay. Even though he said he was okay, I was afraid he was hurting inside. I asked him how he felt.

"Yeah, a couple of the kids on the team were mad at me and griped at me after the game," he said in a disappointed tone. "I actually was going to hold on to the ball, but I had to lunge for it and I thought I was going to fall out of bounds, so I thought I might as well try to get points instead of turn it over."

I thought how Linda has inspired so many people by sharing stories of overcoming adversity. Some of those are her funniest and most impactful stories, because so many people can relate to them. I told Preston the game was something that will probably impact him and was now a part of his story. I told him he may use this someday when he leads others, and it would benefit his team.

On the way home, we bantered about how he could use this story, and had a few laughs with it. The thing is, there was a lot of growth in him that day. He was more engaged in his games the rest of the season. Even though he didn't pursue basketball in high school he took a piece of that experience with him and grew from it.

We are all affected by our personal experiences. Most people pinball through life's experiences, then look up one day to see what they have become. To be a

> *Don't let your experiences define you; define how you use your experiences.*

leader, however, we need to focus proactively on personal growth. Start acting like that person and that leader now. Along the way, consider what's important to you, what your strengths are, what you enjoy, what fulfills you, and what your dreams are. Compare all those things to what you are doing now. There will be failures and successes. But whatever happens, you're in control of developing your story. Don't let your experiences define you; define how you use your experiences.

One last thought:
Once you have developed your story, tell it often. More often than not, you will benefit by people understanding who you are and what your vision is. Think about a leader you admire the most. Did they tell their story? You could probably recite their story to others, couldn't you?

Notes and Insights:

_____

_____

_____

_____

_____

_____

_____

_____

_____

_____

_____

_____

_____

_____

_____

_____

_____

_____

_____

_____

_____

_____

_____

_____

SECTION II: THE LEADER EFFECT

The Leader Effect: The impact of there being a leader. There may be "leadership positions" but it takes someone acting and performing as a leader for there to be a Leader Effect.

CHAPTER 7:
IMPORTANCE OF A LEADER-
SHIP PROCESS

THERE ARE NATURAL BORN LEADERS...then there is me. I grew up a follower. I wasn't even a good follower. I got in line behind whoever I thought was going to help me out the most and then I would be disgruntled the whole time because they weren't meeting my needs. Then I worked my way into a management position and got frustrated people weren't following me. It was not as extreme as it sounds but the point is that before I hit rock bottom, I looked at leadership in terms of leading and following. When I was rebounding, I was learning to lead myself first. Then I noticed others wanting to be a part of what I was doing. I started to look at leadership in terms of joining.

As I meandered through my journey I got the sense people were looking for leaders to join more than follow. Good leaders were attracting, and were thriving with, people who joined rather than

...you can have a profound effect as a leader if you have cultivated something for the people you lead to join...

followed them. This was a transformational shift for me. What do we tend to follow? We tend to follow personality, charisma, style, and influence. What do we tend to join? We tend to join movements, causes, and revolutions. Personality, charisma, style, and influence

71

are alluring, but *focus on the leader*. Regardless of your personality, charisma, style, and influence, you can have a profound effect as a leader if you have cultivated something for the people you lead to join, which *focuses on the team* and the work that needs to be done.

Every leader is going to have strengths and weaknesses. What intrigued me was discovering what commonalities impactful leaders had regardless of their personalities, charisma, style, and influence. How did they build an organization that people wanted to join? What did they look like as a leader? Whereas it is difficult to create a model of personalities, charisma, style, and influence because they vary so much among impactful leaders, we **can** model a leader of a movement, cause, or revolution. I have noticed four motivations for joining an organization throughout my career.

Four Motivations for joining an organization:

- People want to join an organization with purpose and a plan.

- People want to join an organization where they are empowered and prepared.

- People want to join an organization where they are part of a team and where they feel they can contribute.

- People want to join an organization where, personally, they know where they stand, where they can grow, and where they are appreciated.

The key for me was to design a model or process where a leader understood their roles and actions in an organization that people wanted to join. No particular personality, charisma, style, or influence is going to determine success or failure; leadership goes deeper than what we show on the outside.

To design a model, I also had to understand the apparent success of abusive and manipulative people in leadership positions. However, I found that over the long term these methods were tiresome and self-limiting to their teams. In contrast, other leaders who seemed demanding at first could be effective in the long term. The difference is that even seemingly overbearing leaders can gain respect from their teams if they follow a consistent process and focus on serving their team.

I once reported to an executive for whom everything was a crisis. Because this executive *was* clearly in over their head, almost everything was, in fact, a crisis to them. As a matter of routine, they would use phrases like "at all costs," "I don't want to hear that can't be done," "don't make me look bad," "I don't care (about your opinion) ", and "just make this happen." This manager was often condescending and manipulative and was known for taking punitive actions on a whim. It frustrated and stressed our team.

To be clear, any leader may have to play a stern role on some occasions. But a good leader understands and weighs the benefit of the outcome against the consequences of any actions taken. If the building is on fire, you might yell at your team to jump out a second story window to safety, but if you are constantly yelling at your team to jump out a second story window every time they need to leave the building, they will get tired of that.

Leaders adopt this style either as a matter of efficiency or because they lack confidence in their ability to lead. Whereas some leaders have natural talents or were trained well, others find that domination is their most effective resource, backed by their title, or influence. When leaders are constantly in attack mode, their team loses the will for autonomy. And with less autonomy, fewer individuals are empowered to do and think for themselves. This creates more work for the leader—who in turn gets frustrated because he or she is always "putting out fires." Ironically, this person might still be regarded by onlookers as a good leader because of the appearance of control over their people.

Of course, there's the other side of the spectrum as well. Some "leaders" allow team members to push them around and prefer to just let them "manage themselves." There are those who over-analyze everything and reduce their team's efficiency. Others, like the boss I referred to earlier, are overwhelmed and tend to resort to trying not to look bad or wanting their team to make them look good. These are extremes, but I bet you could identify one of these leaders you have had experience with. All these leaders have skills and qualities that could be beneficial, if only they could move beyond making it about them and adopt a consistent leadership process.

The better you understand yourself and your vision, the more inspired a leader you can be. But there's more to being a good leader than your personality, charisma, style, and influence; you still have to know what to do. Developing yourself as a leader requires a purposeful *process*. It helps to have a step by step guide of what to do next as a leader. Enter the FEED Leader. This is a process I developed that focuses on your leadership roles and the actions you should take in those leadership roles. Each phase of FEED Leader focuses on one of the motivations for joining an organization.

Focus: People want to join an organization with purpose and a plan.

Equip: People want to join an organization where they are empowered and prepared.

Execute: People want to join an organization where they are part of a team and where they feel they can contribute.

Debrief: People want to join an organization where, personally, they know where they stand, where they can grow, and where they are appreciated.

FEED Leader

FEED Leader can be used in any situation where you need to lead. It can be personal—for when you need to lead **yourself**—or when you must coach an individual, lead a team, or guide an organization. FEED Leader is the process you use when you are called upon *to lead* an organization people want to join.

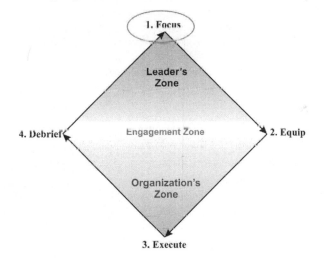

Phase One: **Focus Phase**

The leader always starts here. The Goal of this phase is to Focus or Re-Focus leadership and the team before any action is taken. In this phase, the leader <u>does not engage</u> in the operations of the team. The leadership roles we will be exploring later are:

- The Contemplator

- The Visionary

- The Strategist

- The Planner

- The Coordinator

- The Networker

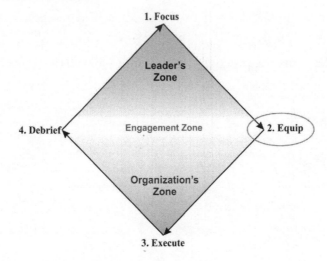

Phase Two: **Equip Phase**

Here, the leader's goal is to proactively prepare the team before any action is taken. In this phase, the leader is <u>fully engaged</u> with the team. The leadership roles we will be exploring later are:

- The Provider

- The Communicator

- The Trainer

- The Coach

- The Model

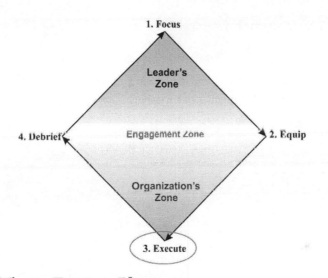

Phase Three: **Execute Phase.**

The goal of this phase is for the team to act autonomously as they are focused and prepared for action. This phase is not in the Leader Zone, which I will explain in more detail next, but the leader does not engage with the team in this phase. The leadership role you will be limited to is:

– The Observer

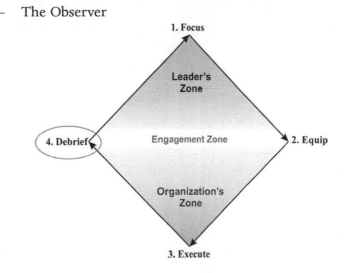

Phase Four: **Debrief Phase.**

The goal of this phase for the leader is to understand the implications of actions taken by the team and to make necessary adjustments. In this phase, the leader is <u>fully engaged</u> with the team. The leadership roles we will be exploring later are:

- The Researcher

- The Collaborator

- The Evaluator

- The Advocate

- The Enforcer

It can be hard to reveal the leader in yourself when you are not confident in your role or the actions you need to take as a leader in certain situations. Knowing and understanding the phases of FEED Leader provides the basis for a sound leadership process and a good guideline to understand your roles and actions. It is also important to understand the Leader's realm. Whether you tend to be more "hands off" or "hands on," a "player's coach" or elusive, confrontational or passive, charismatic or dull, egotistical or humble—you can make leadership work if you know your roles.

Without a process, leaders may only concentrate on their areas of strengths, and completely ignore (or deny) the things they need to improve.

I hope it has become clear why personality, charisma, style, and influence are secondary to having a sound leadership process. FEED Leader can work with a variety of leadership styles and qualities. In fact, working through this process will help leverage your qualities and style. It will encourage you to directly participate in your strong areas and develop or delegate in your weak areas. Without a process, leaders may only concentrate on their areas of strengths, and completely ignore (or deny) the things they need to improve.

Leader's Zone

The realm that leaders are involved in I refer to as the Leader's Zone. This area in FEED Leader includes the Focus Phase, the Equip Phase and the Debrief Phase—the top of the diamond. The Organization's Zone includes the Equip Phase, the Execute Phase and the Debrief Phase—the bottom of the diamond. The zone of engagement happens between the Equip Phase and the Debrief Phase where the leader is fully engaged with the team.

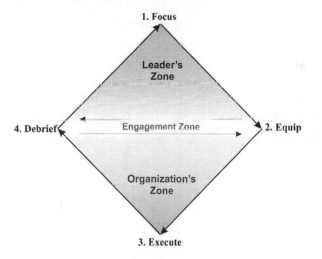

FEED Leader: Leader's Zone and Organization's Zone

This process can break down before you even begin if you don't put early effort into the Focus Phase. A leader needs to own this part. If this is not an area of strength for you, then hire a consultant, engage your leadership team, do research or read, or use a mentor. Find some way to make the Focus Phase the foundation it needs to be.

The Equip Phase is where the leader engages the team—not only by implementing the phase, but by ensuring its effectiveness. Training is part of our Equip Phase. Don't just offer training; make sure the team is learning. You can do this through testing, coaching, or role-playing. If you convey authority to someone in the Equip Phase—and if they stay within the limits of their authority—you must allow them the autonomy to exert their authority, even if it is not exactly how you would do it.

The Debrief Phase gives the leader the chance to learn from the team, and to prepare to return to the Focus Phase. Good engagement in the Debrief Phase also gives the team a sense of ownership in the activity.

It's crucial to understand the leader's roles in the Leader's Zone, since this makes it easier to understand what actions to take. Realize, though, that when you use FEED Leader to lead yourself, you are the team as well as the leader. It is always beneficial to be a FEED Leader at a personal level as you constantly lead yourself. This is where, in your *personal decisions and actions*, you step back in the Focus Phase, you prepare yourself in the Equip Phase, you **take action** in the Execute Phase, and you evaluate yourself in the Debrief Phase.

Linda's business relies heavily on personal business and leadership activities. Linda has become an effective speaker and is asked to speak at various events. Every year, she and I spend time in the Focus Phase to plan out the next year to understand the most effective use of her time as well as her capacity to travel and speak. Anytime there is demand for her time, we go to the Focus Phase and refer to our plan and make a decision. The initial planning is a longer, more thought-out process in the Focus Phase. Once we have a plan, evaluating demand of her time is a quicker process in the Focus Phase.

We also spend time in the Focus Phase as we discuss how she can best prepare her team. This may include plans for coaching, training retreats, communicating, or a pledge to work with someone who is pursuing substantial growth in their business. Then she moves to the Equip Phase as she takes that plan and trains and coaches members of her team. Meanwhile, her team is in the Execute Phase working on their personal business. Linda and I also spend time in the Focus Phase to understand how we are going to look at the data and develop reports to help us track performance. From time to time, Linda and I use these reports to examine her personal business and organization business in the Debrief Phase. Also, in the Debrief Phase, Linda will take time to recognize outstanding performance.

Linda will work with someone in the Debrief Phase to help them understand their business better. Then she will take some time in the Focus Phase to develop a plan to help this person be prepared to use that information in their business. She moves to the Equip Phase to work with this person before they go to the Execute Phase. She may move from the Debrief Phase to the Focus Phase to the Equip Phase in one conversation with this person or it may be spread out over time with many conversations, depending on need. It is important to understand that the key is to know what Phase you are in, what leadership role you need to assume, and the actions you need to take. In a day, you may be moving in and out of leadership roles and handling many different issues. This is when your team sees you being an effective leader.

We will be looking at the leadership roles and actions leaders take in each Phase in the Leader's Zone over the next few chapters. Every leadership role in each phase will need to be filled at one time or another. Be prepared for this! Sometimes you are the best person to fill that role and sometimes you may need to consult with or leverage someone else to fill this role. You don't have to be an expert in every role, just make sure you know where to find the expertise for each role.

The next few chapters are designed to provide practical information regarding FEED Leader and are set up to be useful for reference. It is helpful to see yourself as a leader when you have a concise process to follow on how to act and be seen as a leader.

One last thought:
Ever not know what to do as a leader? Have you wanted to step up as a leader? First thing is to contemplate what phase you need to be in and what role you need to take. If you are not sure, move into the Focus Phase. As you become more aware of what phase of FEED Leader you are in, consider how you feel and if it helps you focus on what you need to do at that moment.

Notes and Insights:

_____

_____

_____

_____

_____

_____

_____

_____

_____

_____

_____

_____

_____

_____

_____

_____

_____

_____

_____

_____

_____

_____

_____

_____

_____

CHAPTER 8: LEADER'S ZONE – FOCUS PHASE

THE LEADER IS ULTIMATELY RESPONSIBLE for their team. President Truman had a sign on his desk that read, "The Buck Stops Here!" He would refer to this sign in speeches or talk about how people wanted to "pass the buck" when taking on issues. But when you are The President, you can't do that. Everything is your responsibility. A President can consult and can even delegate, but the responsibility always ends with them.

So many times, when a "leader" takes action, they are in attack mode. But to maintain consistency, they should be acting within the realm of what they have established in the Focus Phase. What does the situation *actually* look like compared to what it *should* look like? Has the leader set up this team for success? Have they set a standard for excellence? How do they know when they achieve success and excellence? You must use these standards before you act.

Focus means making sure the whole team is moving in the same direction. Success in this Phase increases consistency and reduces distractions. The Focus Phase is a place to solidify Clarity, Belief, and Action Plans. This is paramount as you make key decisions for your team. If the leader is successful in the Focus Phase, their job can be much easier.

It's critical to spend ample time in the Focus phase because you need a period where you are not engaged with the team (as you are during the Equip and Debrief Phase). Some leaders will isolate themselves from the team in the Focus Phase by going on a retreat, either alone or with the leadership team. When should you be in the Focus Phase? The following list provides examples of times when you need to be in the Focus Phase:

- When you are getting ready to start a new business, initiative, product launch, or expansion

- When it is time for personal development or reflection

- When you start to work on annual or long-term plans

- Whenever you need to solve a problem

- When it's apparent there is a systemic issue that needs to be addressed

- When you begin to coach or mentor

- When you are approached for assistance or advice

- When there is a crisis, or a significant win

- Whenever you exit the Debrief Phase

- Anytime you don't know what to do

Focus Phase Leadership Roles:

The Contemplator Role

You may be a person of action, but action is not useful if it lacks purpose. I had worked with an organization where for years a staff member had been compiling information for a monthly mailer. As I began to understand some of the processes of the organization I had trouble identifying exactly why this staff member was performing this task. I had come to learn this exact work was being done by a third party now and the work this staff member was doing was not being used at all. This was a waste of time, energy, and money. Any time in contemplation over the organization would help identify situations like this.

This is a good time to contemplate some questions. What is our core output? How does one decision affect other facets of the operation? Does everything make sense? Is everything happening consistent with what is supposed to be happening? Take the time to contemplate these questions.

The team will be more motivated and productive if they know that leadership is taking time to think about the business and its process. When a staff member is doing work that the organization cannot use, it demonstrates a lack of leadership. The leader's role is to regularly survey the organization's vision and operations. Evidence of this oversight may excite a team by demonstrating progress through awareness and sensibility. The team is better able to focus their efforts when they know someone is putting serious thought into what will bring the entire team success.

Example Actions of the Contemplator:

1. Relax – This is a time to take a deep breath and exude an air of calm.
2. Reflect – All eyes are focused on progress, but the leader needs to look back and understand what happened and why. You can share the lessons learned when you move to the Equip Phase. Even if the organization is in the throes of

production they need the assurance that someone is taking time to consider what happened and why.

3. Think – Brainstorm and run through scenarios in your head. This is a good time to "think out of the box" and test your thoughts. Think about what excellence looks and feels like. How will you measure excellence? What is success, and what will it look and feel like when you achieve it?

The Visionary Role

As my career was developing and we started to solve our personal financial crises, one of the most important things I learned is that nothing shouts "LEADER" more than keeping everyone focused on the vision or purpose. In fact, understanding and applying this concept professionally has helped me focus more in my personal life. During a district sales meeting at Merck, my colleagues and I were discussing some adjustments to our sales objectives that negatively affected some members of our district. What started as one of the many topics on the agenda had ballooned into the main discussion point. Our manager paused the meeting to talk to the team.

"There are two things I can guarantee you. One, there will be negative things that will happen to you that are beyond your control. Two, some of those things are going to be unfair. It's your choice how it affects you. We have a great agenda for this meeting to help you succeed. We can continue with our agenda, or we can continue to gripe."

Your role as a leader is to help your team shed distractions and focus on the vision you created.

This talk served its purpose for our meeting. But it meant so much more to me personally. It was the perspective I needed to shed the guilt and frustration of the crises I was still facing from my earlier trauma of getting my family in a financial crisis. It gave me the permission I needed to focus on the vision I was developing and release the distractions in my life from my past. Your role as a leader is to help your team shed distractions and focus on the vision you created. Think about what distracts your team. Is it social media demands, rumors, potential actions at a higher level in the organization, or something the competition is doing?

Your time in Contemplation should grant you the insight to create the vision for your team. We talked about vision when we discussed personal growth and all the same things apply when it comes to your team. Use CBA for the team and envision your team in a place of "success." Is this where you want to be? Do you feel fulfilled in that place? When you're in the Focus Phase, you're not always developing the vision, but you are always considering it.

Example Actions of The Visionary:

1. Create a vision – Use CBA to understand why you are taking particular actions and what motivates action towards the vision. Using FEED Leader in different scenarios means you are creating a vision for each scenario.

2. Understand the vision – Since you are creating a vision for each scenario, make sure you understand and are consistent with your overarching vision. You may have an overarching vision for the team but a more specific vision for a project. The visions are different but aligned. Aligning visions is important to be aware of because this is where I see a lot of leaders get off track, when the vision of a project doesn't align with the corporate vision.

3. Reflect the vision – You will proactively share the vision in the Equip Phase, but your team should be able to understand the vision by what you say and do. The team should be immersed in the vision, whether or not it is the overarching vision or the vision for a specific project. This is where consistency is born.

The Strategist Role

Once you have spent time in contemplation and developed the vision, you need to devise how that vision can come to fruition. This is the time you choose what to do and what not to do to most effectively and efficiently realize your vision. Strategic thinking is an important role for a leader because it is the basis for all subsequent decisions you will make as a leader.

Developing a strategy is not a one-and-done role. It is a battle between consistency and improvement. Strategies are no more than a continuum of predicted causes and effects. Leaders need to be prepared to evaluate this on a continual basis as tactics are carried out. However, strategies are most effective when played out to the end, so use caution if you need to make adjustments.

It is not always practical or advisable to have everyone *understand* the entire strategy, but it always instills confidence in a leader when a team knows their leader *has* a strategy. As the strategy is executed the team will sometimes have an "Oh, it all makes sense now!" moment while they were focused on their specific tactics.

Example Actions of The Strategist:

1. Collect the facts – Try to avoid a "fragile" strategy whose core is based on too many assumptions. Assumptions are necessary for filling in gaps or predicting cause and effect, but nothing can assure a successful strategy like the facts.

2. Use models   Whatever you are getting ready to do it is inevitable that someone has used that strategy before. Find models of strategies based on your situation and analyze those. This can come from other leaders in your organization, a mentor, or an industry standard. You don't have to mimic the model exactly, but make sure you understand its merits. When Linda and I are discussing her business, we use the term "duplicatable" a lot. When something is working, stick with it.

3. Document your strategy – Whether it is a large-scale initiative like a business plan or a single project, take notes. The smaller the initiative the less formal the strategy needs to be, but documentation has great value. Leaders are going to ask: "Why did you do that?" or "What were you thinking?" We act based on our current frame of mind. Have a plan for enabling your people to have a frame of mind consistent with the strategy by making sure they understand the part of their strategy that is aligned with their plan. When you move into the Debrief Phase, documentation helps to understand what you can do better and what your team can do better.

The Planner Role

It gives the team confidence to know their tasks are part of a plan.

The plan explains how you are going to make the strategy a reality. It is devised of certain action steps or tactics. It gives the team confidence to know their tasks are part of a plan. It may not always be practical to share the strategy throughout, but it is important that you share the plan. The plan is easier to share because it contains defined actions. Bigger and more complex projects may require you to have considered multiple plans to align with the movement of the overall strategy (the typical Plan A, Plan B, etc., scenario). If the plan does change, though, be sure to spend time in the Equip Phase to explain the change. You must be ready to assure the team that they will have all the appropriate resources, training, and support to complete their work and bring the plan to life. Part of this is helping them understand others' roles in the plan.

Example Actions of The Planner:

1. Know the strategy and the vision – This will be very similar to the CBA (Clarity, Belief, Action) action plan. Before you identify the action items or tactics, understand how this plan aligns with the strategy and vision. Find a way to tie each action to the vision.

2. Know your team and resources – Good plans are only good if they *can* work. I hear good leaders talk about setting their teams up for success. This goes back to the plan. Make sure your plan aligns with the skills and interest of your team. Make sure the resources will be available to execute the plan. One of the most impactful movie moments for me was in

Apollo 13. The space shuttle was stranded in space and the crew of the space shuttle had to engage in a lifesaving project by building a filter out of parts on the shuttle. At ground control, they assembled a group of brilliant engineers and told them they had to design and write instructions for this filter. Then someone poured the contents of a box on the table and told the group this was all they could use to design this filter because that was all that was available to the crew on the shuttle. Any one of those engineers could have designed *a* filter in a few minutes. But it took the crew hours to design *the* filter based on the available resources. It can be frustrating for leaders to have to take the time to align resources; most leaders just want it to happen. But, part of leading is knowing your available resources as you make your plan.

3. Design and document a plan – I am going to encourage you to document often. With documentation, you can avoid repeating mistakes, or settle discrepancies on what was understood. The plan should be designed like the CBA Action Plan but with the dynamics of a team working on parts of the plan instead of just an individual. Prepare your plan in a way that you will be able to communicate it well to your team. Plans are not only action plans; they may include organization charts, budgets, or any other planning decisions that need to be made for the organization or the initiative.

The Coordinator Role

You may find that not everything fits neatly into your plans, and that's okay. You can either push forward, having confidence in your plan, or you can make adjustments. The Coordinator's role in the Focus Phase is to implement, evaluate, adjust, and reassign resources in the plan. The process and results of the Coordinator constitute the most visible role of the leader in the Focus Phase. You might see the Coordinator role when a football coach is studying the plays on a card during a game, or when a basketball coach huddles with the other coaches before he addresses the team. Of all the leader roles in the Focus Phase, this is the role that requires you to "think on your feet" the most.

Example Actions of The Coordinator:

1. Ad hoc resource assignments – Even though people are in place and resources assigned, things arise that were not part of the plan. A leader needs to know how to stay consistent with the strategy and make adjustments.

2. Clear a path – Just like the Planner, The Coordinator needs to be consistent in setting the team up for success. This action refers to the fact that whether things are following the plan or if it is ad hoc, you can continuously foster a successful work environment. Remember, we are in the Focus Phase, so this has to do with things like making sure there are funds available, there are contingency plans, there is talent, there is adequate infrastructure, and so on—things that need to happen before you engage the team.

3. Take initiative – I picture the leader in a Coordinator Role when there is a crisis. As soon as the crisis hits, the leader

is quickly thinking of the best solution, resources needed, and actions that should be taken. Then the leader moves quickly into the Equip Phase to assign people to tasks. There doesn't need to be a crisis for you to switch to the Coordinator Role, but take the initiative when you do need to make adjustments.

The Networker Role

A core role during the Focus Phase is to understand what is happening externally around your team. Most CEOs are engaged with and communicate with other CEOs. They have positions in organizations and associations that affect their industry.

When companies look at bringing people into leadership positions, they consider their experience in the whole environment around their job. Merck typically hired from within and usually required those who would lead others to have two or three various positions within the company first for this reason. It enriches Linda's business that so many leaders in the organization have such diverse experiences and backgrounds. There is always someone who can relate to any situation her team runs into. Whether it is external or internal, leaders spend time sharing their experiences with each other that provides valuable resources to their team. Linda is well known for her "I know a guy" moments. Like, "I know a guy who can print those cheap," or "I know a guy who has experience with that." Good leaders have a good leader network.

Example Actions of The Networker:

1. Being out and about – Even though being a leader is very rewarding and an integral part of personal fulfillment, no one ever said it is always fun. As a networker it is important to be out there so your team is always connected. Some of us enjoy networking, but whether you enjoy it or not, you need to make yourself available to others outside your team, and I'm not referring just to the fun parts. Stretch yourself to be more out there. This may include serving on boards, attending events, and taking late night calls. However, you should never compromise your morals or integrity to add to your network, even if it costs you an opportunity.

2. Give and take – We addressed this in personal growth; networking is a servant's role. The approach is not to get what you can out of people but to engage with others to the benefit of all involved.

3. Develop external relationships – Rarely does a team thrive without impacting or being impacted by others outside the team. Whether you work with other leaders within your organization, within your industry, or outside your industry, these relationships build a robust human resource for your team. Understand that it may not always be you personally who takes on these responsibilities, but it is your responsibility to be sure these relationships are developed.

World War II is the last war the United States was involved in that seemed to have a universal sense of purpose and cause. This by no means diminishes the valor and commitment of the men and women who have served on foreign shores since that war. It does speak to our perception of that war and the leaders who made a lasting impression. We learn about generals who were seen as extraordinary leaders. When you reflect on the roles of the leader in the Focus Phase, envision a World War II general leading a military endeavor.

Think about all the work you would expect that general to do before any troops hear or see him—the time he would spend in the Contemplator Role understanding the significance of the situation and weighing the impact of any action needed. He would need foresight in the Visionary Role as he sees what victory means to the world. Time would need to be spent in evaluating of the causes and effects in the Strategist Role. Resources would need to be considered and planned in the Planner Role. As the war went on, the general would be involved in constant maneuvering in the Coordinator Role. All the while he would be building alliances and negotiating with other stakeholders in the Networker Role. Even though the troops don't actively see him in the Focus Phase, they see his leadership from being in the Focus Phase.

It reminds me of a quote from General Douglas MacArthur: *"A true leader has the confidence to stand alone, the courage to make tough decisions and the compassion to listen to the needs of others. He does not set out to be a leader but becomes one by the equality of his actions and the integrity of his intent."* General MacArthur is describing moments in the Focus Phase.

One last thought:
The Focus Phase is the essence of effective leadership. Where does your mind go when faced with a leadership situation? What did others do or need to do in that situation? Try starting in the Focus Phase where you evaluate your leadership first to give parameters on what you do next.

Notes and Insights:

CHAPTER 9:
LEADER'S ZONE – EQUIP PHASE

THE BIGGEST TRANSITION I HAD to make going from a small company I owned and operated to a Fortune 500 company like Merck was to understand the resources available. My first manager at Merck appreciated that I approached my job as entrepreneur. It also drove him crazy. Not only did I run my territory like a business; I also tried to handle every situation myself.

Merck spent an enormous amount of time and resources training us on products, selling, customer management, and resources. We studied, took tests, role-played, listened to lectures, practiced, and met support staff for several weeks preparing for our jobs. Managers would coach and model selling skills and managing administrative tasks when we were working in the field. Even though they prepared us thoroughly, it took me a while to start utilizing the resources. Once I learned to be taught by and rely on others, I thought I would never work for a small company again—couldn't imagine working without all these resources at my fingertips.

The Equip Phase is a phase I see neglected or underperformed often—and each time that happens leaders are perplexed why things didn't work out. What I have learned from leaders is how critical it is for every team member to be thoroughly prepared. The Equip Phase can seem like an annoyance to some leaders because they're so eager for the team to execute. However, it's more annoying when you are relying on someone to perform and they are not prepared.

Whereas the leader has limited engagement with the team during the Focus Phase, there is significant engagement during the Equip Phase. When should you be in the Equip Phase? The following list offers some examples:

- When you need to share your vision

- When you are ready to implement a new plan

- When you need to motivate and inspire your team

- When you need to train a skill or procedure

- When you start engaging in coaching or mentoring

- When you need to provide resources

- When you need to share expectations

- When you need to teach principles and standards

Equip Phase Roles:

The Provider Role

One area that falls squarely on the leader's shoulders is assuring all appropriate resources are assigned to the team. Even though the leader can delegate this task, it is still ultimately his or her responsibility. You want to avoid a situation where your team takes action and falls short of expectations—simply because they didn't have the resources they needed. You plan for all of this

> *One way to keep a team content and motivated is to keep them confident in the fact that they will always have the tools they need to do their jobs.*

during the Focus Phase but need to make sure you *supply* it in the Equip Phase. One way to keep a team content and motivated is to keep them confident in the fact that they will always have the tools they need to do their jobs.

Example Actions of The Provider:

1. Procurement/Hiring – Based on your strategy and plan, you understand your objectives and what resources you need to meet those objectives. Now it is time to act and develop the infrastructure, obtain the tools, and place people in the right positions.

2. Provide access to resources – The actions of the provider are much more practical in nature than some of the other roles in The Equip Phase. However, one challenge in this role is the continual effort to make sure that all your personnel have access to the resources you have trained them on. Resources include (to name a few):

   - Funding

   - Authority

   - Tools

   - Personnel

   - References/Procedures

   - Certifications/Licenses

   - Information

   - Technology

It's easy to set expectations and not think through if your team has access to all the resources they need to meet those expectations.

3. Be a buffer – Sometimes the action of the Provider is to provide a buffer for your team to keep them focused. Sometimes it is from conflicting messages from higher management. Other times you take the criticism and filter it to your team in the debrief phase. There may be times you let your team vent and then take the responsibility to research their issues and concerns, so they can focus on production.

The Communicator Role

The primary and simplest role of the leader during the Equip Phase is that of a communicator. You determine what you need to communicate during the Focus Phase; the Equip Phase demands that you take action and communicate based on your plan. Teams can experience a great deal of angst when they receive inconsistent communication or none at all—especially if some members do not feel they are being communicated to while others do.

This is a balancing act. I want to encourage you to be prolific in your communication, but also to use discretion. Fully open communication and transparency in an organization can cause tremendous distractions. The following guidelines can help determine whether you should share information with your team members or not:

1. If you're still working out the details of a topic in the Focus Phase, then it probably is not ready for mass consumption. Otherwise, you need to be prepared to update everyone every

time ideas change. Of course, this may not be practical. This is different from purposefully consulting with team members on specific details in the Focus Phase, which can be necessary. However, most feedback will come from the Debrief Phase.

2. Sometimes there is sensitive or proprietary information that is discussed amongst leadership. It is important to track and monitor who needs and has this information so great care should be taken in how this information is communicated.

3. The purpose of communication is to give people the appropriate amount of information they need to do their job. Too much information can be distracting, while too little information can hinder performance. Sometimes information is "too big" to comprehend, meaning it is not practical to explain the context or background. Establish a relationship with your teams so they understand there will be times, not too often though, that they need to act on pieces of information even though they do not understand the full context.

4. Communication and trust go hand in hand. Most times communicate freely and often with your teams. However, in times when you need to hold back information or only partially communicate information, always let your team know up front that you are only giving them the information they need to do their job. Bottom line: give your team what they need to understand the vision, do their job, and feel included. Be honest and consistent in the process.

Example Actions of the Communicator:

1. Communicate – Once you decide what needs to be communicated you cannot communicate too much. Communicate both orally and in writing. Oral communication conveys emotion and tone. Written communication provides a record and details that are remembered easier.
2. Be accessible – As with networking, being accessible is the best way to assure there is active and accurate communication.
3. Inspire and Motivate – This is not unique to The Communicator, but it is an integral action for this role. Leaders in Linda's organization often say they train the heart as well as the head and hands.

The Trainer Role

This might be the most obvious role of a leader in the Equip Phase, because it tends to be a formal process in preparing people to do their job. However, understand that training is not simply providing the tools and processes for teaching skills. It includes ensuring that everyone is learning what they need to know to be prepared. While the leader may not personally provide training, their role is to make sure training is comprehensive.

Example Actions of The Trainer:

1. Teaching – As a continuation of communication there is a time that your team is learning information for the first time. Whether it is technical skills, policies and procedures, processes, etc., this is where you are introducing information.

2. Simulation – Once information is taught, a trainer uses various tools to help their team understand how to use the information. This is a creative aspect of the role where you implement role-playing, practice, and supervised activities.

3. Testing – The wrong place to learn if your team understands what you are training is when it is time to execute. Testing can be formal or informal. The point is to provide assurances that the objective of the training is accomplished.

4. Inspire and Motivate – This is an action in other Equip Phase roles as well, but training is a great opportunity to inspire your team. Try not to think of inspiration as a tingly feeling in their belly but an affirmation of action needed. When an artist or writer is inspired they go from a state of not knowing what to paint or write to a state of knowing exactly what to paint or write. Your team should be motivated from that same process when they leave the Equip Phase.

The Coach Role

Sometimes the most productive work in the Equip Phase is done in the conversations that take place in the days and weeks after training. By this time, the team has had a chance to implement their training; they now need motivation, clarification, or more instruction. Typically, though, coaching is not practical unless the team or individual has exerted some effort to work. Coaching is part of the Equip Phase, preparing your team for execution. We will discuss discipline and correction in the Debrief Phase.

Example Actions of The Coach:

1. Gaining mutual consent – When I use the word "coaching" I get two distinct reactions. The first reaction is the assumption that it is a disciplinary action or performance remediation. We'll discuss this in the Debrief Phase. The second reaction is what I am referring to here and that is regarding development and growth. For this definition, if there is not mutual consent on meeting and improving, then your role is more of a trainer than a coach. Trust has to be at the foundation of coaching.

2. Listen – A key aspect of coaching is understanding why you are coaching. Be aware that your initial impression of each person on your team or the objective for coaching might not be the reality.

3. Probe – If you are going to take the time to coach, use this time to learn more about your subject and their needs. There may be some crossover here with roles in The Debrief Phase, but The Coach Role is focused on preparing your team for The Execute Phase.

4. Set personal objectives – Once you understand the true purpose of coaching, make sure you are clear on the objective of coaching.

5. Implement CBA – Coaching is a great opportunity to use Clarity, Belief and Action to accomplish the objective (as discussed in Chapter 4).

The Model Role

The last thing a leader wants to be is counterproductive. My son is wicked smart and has an intelligent sense of humor. Preston can be a clever practical joker and likes to mess with people's heads sometimes. Fortunately, he is usually pretty funny and innocuous. But when he was much younger, I would have to caution him or ask him to stop joking around from time to time. He never intentionally did anything annoying, but sometimes his antics wasted people's time; they either had to clean something up, redo work, or it would simply break their concentration. Most people get very annoyed when they realize they have wasted time.

When leaders don't model what they communicate, train, or coach, it can diminish their efforts to prepare their team. They have wasted their own time. Part of equipping your team is *demonstrating* what they need to learn. If you communicate that integrity is the highest priority but your team sees you taking liberties on your expense report they will have trouble believing integrity is your highest priority. However, if you train them that teamwork is critical, and they see you going out of your way to help a team member, it reinforces that practice.

> *When leaders don't model what they communicate, train or coach, it can diminish their efforts to prepare their team.*

Modeling motivation, behavior, or techniques can be the difference between success and failure moving into the Execute Phase.

Example Actions of The Model:

1. Know principles and standards – You spend time in the Focus Phase establishing policies, standards and principles of the team. Make sure you know and understand these, so you can be sure to model them.

2. Act with integrity – If you want your team to act with integrity then you must demonstrate that to them, not only in matters of character but also integrity to the processes and skills. *Your team will learn more from your behavior than anything you have told them.*

3. Be visible – Akin to "Be available," being in the presence of your team gives them a reference for expectations. Sometimes you cannot physically be "visible" to your team all the time based on the nature of your organization, but, letting them know you are around through technology and social media gives them the model they need. The point is not to be a "hovering" presence but visible enough to fill the gaps of their understanding of what they need to do.

Being a parent has many challenges. Now that my children are in high school and college we sometimes discuss aspects of their rearing and I often mention to them that parents don't have an instruction manual specific for each child. Knowing I wasn't going to be the perfect parent, my main objective was to make sure my kids were prepared to have as many opportunities available to them as possible. The Roles of the Equip Phase remind me of the roles we have as parents as our kids develop into adulthood.

Even though a leader would not be respected if they treated their teams like children, the roles of the Equip Phase, at a fundamental level, are similar to our roles as parents. Both parents and leaders provide basic needs in the Provider Role. We start explaining things and setting expectations in the Communicator Role. In the Trainer Role, we show how things work and let them practice and experiment in a controlled environment. We are letting them do things on their own and giving guidance as needed in the Coach Role. And we are constantly in the Model Role, where we have to be sure what we do is consistent with what we say and teach.

When you are preparing your team, imagine that your parents told you as a five-year-old that you were responsible for preparing your own meals. What if you told your ten-year-old son or daughter they needed to get a job and support themselves? That is extreme, but sometimes we expect things from those we lead before they are prepared to execute those expectations. People will see a good leader in you if you spend the necessary time and effort in the Focus Phase and thoroughly prepare your team in the Equip Phase. As a reminder, you can be a leader in the Focus Phase and the Equip Phase even if you don't have a title or an official leadership position. These are just things leaders do.

One last thought:
Don't neglect the Equip Phase. You can't have expectations in the Execute Phase if you did not prepare in the Equip Phase. Have you ever gone straight from planning to execution? It is an easy tendency to do, especially for routine or minimal tasks. In sports, coaches will caution their players with "don't overlook this opponent," meaning they should prepare as if it is their most difficult opponent.

Notes and Insights:

_____
_____
_____
_____
_____
_____
_____
_____
_____
_____
_____
_____
_____
_____
_____
_____
_____
_____
_____
_____
_____
_____
_____
_____
_____
_____
_____
_____

Chapter 10: Leader's Zone – Debrief Phase

(Be aware that we are staying in the Leader's Zone and
skipped the Execute Phase for now.)

YOU ALL HAVE AN AREA of strength that bolsters the leader in
you. Find out what that strength is and leverage it as you grow as a
leader. One thing I was recognized for when I started my career with
Merck was my analytical skillset. After working in sales, I progressed
to analyst positions. I worked as a Senior Sales Analyst and team
leader developing analytic tools for the sales force before I advanced
into management. It's probably my analyst perspective that prompts
me to emphasize this crucial Phase to FEED Leader. Each role has
such an important function. However, if you find you are having
trouble making progress or dealing with the same issues year after
year, try spending more time in the Debrief Phase. Once you cycle
back through to this phase again you shouldn't be dealing with the
same issues.

This is the time to get feedback from the team in a productive and
positive way. It is also a chance for the leader to evaluate and provide
team feedback. Team members expect this of a leader, and it's always
refreshing when leaders consider feedback and make appropriate

changes. But this doesn't happen unless you are earnest in your Debrief Phase efforts. You want to put mechanisms in place when moving from the Focus Phase through the Execute Phase to collect data and create information that everyone can use to evaluate performance. In the Equip Phase, you test and document your planning and decision-making from the Focus Phase. In the Execute Phase, you test and document your preparation and resource allocation from the Equip Phase. After the Execute Phase, the leader evaluates all pertinent information collected before spending time in the Focus Phase again.

The Debrief Phase involves in-depth engagement with your team. Not only are you evaluating, you are interacting with the team to help them understand their performance and where they stand with you as the leader. Whereas you will be moving back to the Focus Phase, from here your team will be moving on to the Equip Phase. There is a transition for the interaction with the team I want to describe here to emphasize the fluid movement between the Debrief and Equip Phase. *This is a transition from informing and evaluating to preparing for execution.*

In the Debrief Phase you may be rewarding or correcting a behavior, then moving to the Equip Phase where you will be training or coaching based on the Debrief Phase evaluation. This distinction is a dividing line for your interaction with the team between being reactive to being proactive. *It is always important to have your team moving into action from a proactive position, which is coming from the Equip Phase.* The Debrief Phase is a reactive position to help everyone understand what has happened.

When should you be in the Debrief Phase? The following are some examples:

– When you need to evaluate performance

- When you need to correct behavior

- When you want to reward or recognize behavior or accomplishment

- When you need to gather internal data and information about operations

- When expectations are not being met

- When it is time for scheduled review of operations and performance

- When you need to intervene during the Execute Phase, at which point you move to The Debrief Phase

Leaders don't disappear when the team is in the Execute Phase, however. They are always observing and collecting information. The Debrief Phase is a continual, formal process with scheduled benchmarks. A good leader also has a general understanding of the climate in between the benchmarks. I was told once that litigating lawyers are trained never to ask a question where they don't already know how the witness will answer. In the Debrief Phase that isn't quite true, but almost. If you wait for benchmarks to review progress you might not like what you find out.

Debrief Phase Roles

The Researcher Role

Sometimes leaders can be overly confident in how much they understand their team and operations. My philosophy is to be as prepared as I can with all the information—but teach the team to be proactive in providing feedback. You *may* actually know everything that is going on, but odds are you will gain an important perspective from the individuals you're leading if they are your researchers and analysts, especially if you train them to come to you with honest and timely assessments.

This role includes gathering data and opinions, collating information, and studying reports. Having generated and collected data, leaders need to invest resources to analyze it; otherwise, it is hard to see progress. If you want your team to be proactive in this role, make sure they know how to gather information and analyze it (Equip Phase). Some data are quantitative, which means they include numbers that you can calculate to analyze performance. This would include things like the time it takes to produce a number of products or evaluating if you sold more or less of a product this quarter over last quarter. Some data are qualitative, derived from observation and opinions. This would be information like if workers say they are happier now than last year or if the team seems to be more motivated.

You should have already established in the Focus Phase what information is valuable to analyze performance and put steps in place to ensure you're collecting that data. While you want to gather and keep as much data as you can for further research, you must also have a plan for what you need, and for what you're going to do with the reports. You don't want to fall victim to "analysis paralysis"—that is, spending so much time in the data and information that you never take any action.

Example Actions of The Researcher:

1. Gather data and opinions – In the Focus Phase you should establish what information you need to gather. Develop the

mechanisms to collect this information through the Equip and Execute Phases.

2. Analyze – Analysis does not have to be complicated. It is just a matter of making sure you understand the relevant information.

3. Make reports – Make sure you and your team have access to reporting. You want to be prepared for evaluating and to challenge your team's self-assessments.

The Collaborator Role

Collaboration is a common theme throughout the Debrief Phase, but it has its own specific role in this phase. Communicate to the team the expectations in the Equip Phase, and make information on performance available to them. As a leader, you know and analyze the information on performance; however, let the team collaborate with you and approach you with information on what went well and what needs improvement. Teams that do this well will find that as time goes on, they're able to make corrections in real time and resolve potential setbacks before outcomes are determined. At the same time, the team takes ownership of their actions and helps provide solutions.

This requires the Leader to establish a safe environment for honest discourse. Mistakes and misjudgments happen and need to be addressed judiciously as part of the process. Just remember, when expectations aren't met you have to look at the leader in the Focus Phase and the Equip Phase before you look at the team in Execute Phase. A safe environment is one where the team is not threatened, attacked, or manipulated to be anything but honest and forthcoming.

> *What has happened can't change but what you do moving forward can change the impact of what has happened.*

Unfortunately, sometimes the way things are presented is not always how things really are. I've seen my share of those in positions of responsibility creating deceptive narratives for others that matched the desired outcome when serious vulnerabilities needed to be addressed that weren't. They didn't feel they could give an honest assessment of performance and still win approval. Of course, this doesn't serve anyone in the long run. Leaders should encourage honesty during setbacks. Leaders should accept a respectful dissenting voice, critical opinion, or disappointing results in the Debrief Phase. What has happened can't change, but what you do moving forward can change the impact of what has happened. Everything must be on the table for best results.

This happens at all levels of severity and sometimes maybe seem innocuous. Sometimes the biggest disasters started as an inconsequential manipulation to make things seem better than they were. One of the biggest corporate and financial scandals that I can remember was when the Wall Street darling, Enron, went bankrupt around 2002. The crux of the issue? Hiding information about debt to increase their value. What could have been just a setback to the company on the onset, if reported correctly, turned into the downfall of several companies with billions of dollars lost and thousands of people losing their livelihood.

A successful Debrief Phase hinges on communication and tone. You want to have mechanisms in place to ensure that open communication happens consistently and in a timely manner. The most effective tone here expresses desire for success for each team member as well as the team as a whole. *In the Debrief Phase, bosses can demean their team, when it would be better to empower them.*

Whereas you are working with your team towards an action when coaching in the Equip Phase, in the Debrief Phase you're acting as collaborator, and focused on getting the best information. Similar to coaching, collaboration means you need to eliminate as many preconceptions of your people and of the situation as possible. It's critical to work with your teams to gain understanding before you draw any conclusions.

This is why I prefer to create an environment where the team takes control of this phase. They can study the information, draw from their experience in the trenches, and come to conclusions that you can compare to your own observations from your perspective. There is value in relying on our teams as experts in their jobs.

From here you take your findings to the Focus Phase, to prepare for the Equip Phase, and to the next roles in the Debrief Phase. *You shouldn't go through the FEED Leader cycle again and end up with the same issues you had the first time in Debrief Phase.* If you have an annual meeting and you are lamenting the same issues you were last year, then you need to take a serious look at your efforts in the Leader's Zone.

Example Actions of The Collaborator:

1. Make yourself accessible – Sometimes we think the thing we are doing is the most important thing happening. It reminds me of the parent-child scenario almost all of us have experienced or seen:
   Child: "Mom."
   Mom: "Just a minute, I'm trying to find my keys"
   Child: "Mom!"
   Mom: "Hold on! I've got to find my keys."
   Child: "But Mom!"

Mom: *agitated* "Will you leave me alone! I have to find my keys! We are going to be late if I don't find them right now!"

Child: "Mom!"

Mom: "WHAT!!!"

Child: "Junior has your keys in his mouth!"

Being accessible means the leader submits to the team and places everyone on equal footing while you all try to come to the best solutions.

2. Inquire – This role requires you to probe, ask questions, and listen. Lead the discussion, don't dominate it.

The Evaluator Role

After the Collaborator Role, you should have reasonable information and perspectives to evaluate your people and the situation. Ambitious teams are always anxious to have their performance evaluated. This is not a time to slip into an authority mode unless a critical and urgent matter needs to be addressed. Similar to the Research Role, training the team to self-evaluate gives you an additional perspective in this role. Effective evaluation is an examination through the entire FEED Leader process from your own performance in Focus Phase, to the effectiveness of the Equip Phase, to the accomplishments of the Execute Phase.

Example Actions of The Evaluator:

1. Engagement – This entire phase is about engaging with the team, but as the Evaluator, there is an official team interaction. This is where the team gets an understanding of what you are thinking and where they stand with you. As you have probably experienced, each individual on the team

is continuously trying to get a feel for the opinion of their leadership on their value.

2. Communicate – There is nothing much worse than an "evaluation" from a leader where you walk away and wonder where you stand and what you are supposed to do. If you follow the FEED Leader, the communication in this role should be evident. Regardless, communication should be straightforward and actionable. To improve, there has to be friction, and sometimes that comes through evaluations. Also, communication has to come from you, the leader, with no leaks and no indirect communications.

3. Document – The evaluation is the process of formulating final assessments or making judgements. These determinations are going to be valuable in the Focus Phase and the Equip Phase, so they must be documented and retained as benchmarks and data for future research.

The Advocate Role

The key function of this role is to recognize and reward your team to encourage desired behavior. When a team feels confident their leader is looking for ways to elevate them and be their advocate, it incentivizes them. You can practice this often: at home with your kids, with a social group, a sports team—any situation where you want to encourage a behavior. Remember, it doesn't matter whether you are designated as a leader or not; you can always be an active advocate.

> *When a team feels confident their leader is looking for ways to elevate them and be their advocate, it incentivizes them.*

Recognizing excellence reinforces excellence and demonstrates a model for behavior. This is where you can strengthen behavior based on established standards. However, you risk impacting the team negatively if recognition and rewards are arbitrary, or if the process is not transparent. Consistent and sincere recognition of success can mitigate negative outcomes or behavior. People want to be acknowledged for their efforts. They will change their behavior to be involved in that culture.

Varying the recognition can give leaders the flexibility to drive outcomes and behavior that are most critical to the team. You might identify one desired behavior with a simple acknowledgement in front of peers and upper management, or recognize consistent, valuable outcomes with a plaque or certificate. Leadership might even give a monetary reward for a significant success or for consistent behavior. If you give the team a variety of recognitions to look forward to, you give them a variety of ways to contribute. The more liberal leaders are with recognition, the more eagerly team members will strive for outcomes and behavior that receive that appreciation. Keep in mind that the recognition needs to be sincere, genuine, and appropriate. *It can be demotivating to receive recognition that is contrived.*

Example Actions of The Advocate:

1. Know your goals – This action draws from the work you did in the Focus Phase where you identified the actions you want to reward based on your goals. Know what these goals are to help assure consistent recognition.

2. Recognize and reward – Take time to recognize and reward behavior and outcomes that you desire. Make this as public as possible, and include prominent members of the

organization. You will probably notice more organic peer-to-peer recognition as you continue this practice.

3. Speak well of your team – Literally, be an advocate. When your team hears from others that their leader has good things to say about them, it adds a level of sincerity. However, be genuine as an advocate. Your team has to reconcile what you are saying about them to how you act towards them and to what they know about themselves.

The Enforcer Role

You get significantly more mileage in your role as Advocate than you do as Enforcer, but it is important to take on this role when necessary. Distinguish this role from the one we take in the Equip Phase, where you are looking to improve skills, increase attention to details, or ensure appropriate decision-making. You have to become the Enforcer when you need to call attention to urgent or critical problems. Sometimes abrupt punitive action is needed in cases of safety, liability, or a risk to the culture. This is where you notice a trend or willful disregard that you need to correct.

However, it is best to follow up Enforcer actions and move to the Equip Phase with coaching or training back through the Execute Phase and on to the Debrief Phase where you can recognize and reward improvements. The Enforcer Role is probably the least enjoyable role for the Leader to fill—but a strong leader will fill it when they need to. A team will respect a leader who assumes the Enforcer Role at the appropriate time.

When leaders need to use Debrief for correction, they must base this on established standards. This helps ensure consistency and fairness. Take personal feelings out of the equation. When outcomes or behavior fall short of expectations, leaders should communicate with as much vigor as recognition—but in private (with few exceptions, such as suppressing systemic insubordination by taking an example punitive action towards one individual or group). Give the individual or team the benefit of taking ownership of their shortfall and the correction, thereby aiding their personal growth.

It's critical to identify whether the substandard performance was a rare one-time event, or if it's becoming a trend. Once this is determined, you can evaluate and make decisions during the Focus Phase including proper placement, resources provided, or separation. You can also apply corrective actions in Equip, such as changing positions, providing different resources, or offering more training.

Example Actions of The Enforcer:

1. Identify behavior to correct – This role is focused on personnel. What we want to identify is behavior or outcomes that are more systemic than inadvertent. They may have to do with the character of an individual or the ability of an individual that doesn't seem self-corrective.

2. Confront – In this role more interactions are going to be more confrontational than in any other role. Keep in mind that the tone should always be one of wanting to help, while making it clear that there are consequences to certain behaviors.

3. Support – Check your emotions before you take on this role. There is nothing wrong with being stern, but if you are going to have impact you cannot get personal. The focus is always on actions you are trying to correct, not the person who performed them. It can get more personal when you move to the Equip Phase, but only in a productive way.

It is probably clear now that I enjoy sports. Whether I was watching or playing, sports were probably 80% of my childhood, outside of school. When I watch professional football, I am always intrigued with what Mondays after the Sunday games look like. This is the ultimate Debrief Phase experience.

I understand professional football teams are loaded with analytics. I always wonder what the coaches are doing in the Researcher Role when they engage the broader home office team to get information they need to move through the Debrief Phase. Even though Coaches are involved in the Focus Phase and the Equip Phase the day after games, they also engage the team in the Collaborator Role as they work with the players to assess what happened during the game.

Different from the proactive engagement in the Equip Phase, the coaches react to stats and film in the Evaluator Role to inform the players where they stand with the coaches. They also spend time in the Advocate Role as they reward and recognize players with game balls or other recognition. But they are also notorious for their interaction with the players in the Enforcer Role as they try to correct poor play or poor effort.

Sports teams are highly recognized for their practice-then-play process. That process is developed by what happens in the Debrief Phase throughout the week.

Be Aware of No Activity

FEED Leader is based on action. Beware of the antithesis of FEED Leader: *no action*. You may have the best Debrief process imaginable, but quickly realize that you have nothing to evaluate. This tends to happen when real work is not being performed. This is very apparent in some positions; in others it's harder to identify. Some team members excel at making their job look "busy" when in fact they aren't being productive. This might have more to do with lax Leadership than a team member's willingness though.

Every leader needs the Debrief Phase, not only to look at the positive and negative feedback, but also to recognize situations with little or no feedback to rely on. If you are not prepared for this scenario, it is easy for it to go unnoticed, and then you wonder why your corrective measures aren't effective. Use FEED Leader to drive *action!*

The key to FEED Leader is understanding your roles and actions in the Leader Zone. Practice FEED Leader in the Leader's Zone and you will start to see who you are as a leader. Following a leadership process helps you understand your leadership strengths and weaknesses. At the same time, it guides you through the process of being a leader. Tune your engine, check the restraints, and polish the car. The leader in you is really showing.

One last thought:
In the Focus Phase you design; in the Equip Phase you prepare; in the Execute Phase the organization acts; and in the Debrief Phase you compare what things look like against the design, the preparation, and the action.

Notes and Insights:

CHAPTER 11:
OUTSIDE THE LEADER'S
ZONE – EXECUTE PHASE

HAVE YOU EVER NOTICED A leader that seems to have the appropriate reaction to *any* situation? This happens when a leader is keenly aware of their current role and the actions needed.

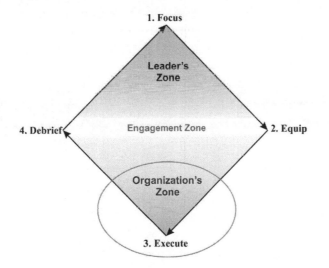

We skipped over the FEED Leader Execute Phase because, as a leader, you do not have an active role in that phase. Sometimes you can observe and collect data in the Execute Phase, but this is not practical for some leaders. This phase falls outside the Leader's Zone. Most of your time should be spent in the Leader's Zone where you will engage with the team in the Equip Phase and Debrief Phase or separate yourself in the Focus Phase. If you are involved in the Execute Phase, consider yourself part of the team in the Organization's Zone. Then you have a clear distinction when you need to move back to the Leader's Zone. This is similar to how a sports coach is involved in games by calling plays as part of the organization, but then transitions to the Leader's Zone to make adjustments (Focus Phase), teach (Equip Phase) or reward and rebuke (Debrief Phase) while the game is in progress.

Unless you are part of a large organization, you are likely to find yourself with roles in the Execute Phase in team operations. Your *leadership* in regard to operations is the impact you have in equipping and debriefing—not by performing operations tasks. Linda spends time doing activities that are part of working her personal business; this is time she spends in the Organization's Zone. When she starts developing and preparing her people, she is in the Leader's Zone. Understanding the distinction of what Zone you are in can really help you function as a leader. When you're a leader and are part of the team in operations, there are certain dynamics you need to consider.

1. You have the same boss as everyone else on your team. It may be you, in which case you need to emulate how you want others to respond to your leadership. No shortcuts just because you're the boss. If the boss is someone else, then you need to submit to their authority.

2. When you need to step in and engage with your team as a leader, then you need to clearly occupy the Leader's Zone in the Equip or Debrief Phase.

I have seen so many leaders get bogged down not understanding their position when it comes to their role in operations.

An example of a leader who also works in the Organization's Zone may be a mechanic who owns a shop. This mechanic has responsibilities for leading and for his role in operations. He is the leader *and* part of the team. He may be the best mechanic in the world where he can lead by example—but his business will not be successful unless he leads the organization when he plans, prepares, and evaluates his team in the Leader's Zone.

However, if he is working as part of the team he needs to work as hard as he can on his tasks. This can be a quandary when he has Execute Phase tasks while he is trying to be a planner or trainer. Understand your role in any situation and know the actions you need to take in that role. Understand, also, that the next moment may find you in another situation in another role, maybe part of the team in the Organization's Zone.

In the Leader's Zone, this shop owner might be in the Planner Role in the Focus Phase in his office making sure he has enough inventory or the right equipment to service the number of cars he plans to work on. He may move into the Coach Role in the Equip Phase to help a new mechanic realize how he could use some new equipment more efficiently. This, following a discussion yesterday with him in the Evaluator Role in the Debrief Phase on how he is taking too long with a certain type of repair.

Soon after that, a long-time customer comes in for an appointment and is expecting the shop owner to work on their car personally, so he is now part of the team in the Execute Phase. When he is done working on that car he might move back to the Leader's Zone to check back with the new employee in the Collaborator Role in the Debrief Phase to get feedback on how he is doing with the new equipment.

To look at this another way, a lot of organizations don't make a clear distinction between Equip "practice time" and Execute "game time." When is an accountant in practice time or game time? Understand when you and your team are preparing for action and when you and your team are performing an action. In preparation, the leader is engaged with the team in the Equip Phase. In performing, it is up to the team to act in the Execute Phase. When you, as the leader, are part of performing, then you are part of the team in the Execute Phase.

While the team is in the Execute Phase, the leader's role feels like most parents do when their kids are in a performance, public speaking, or sports. In eighth grade, my daughter was a candle-lighter in the middle school National Honor Society induction ceremony. Each candle- lighter had to read a short text before he or she lit their candle. Sarah had memorized hers, and when she went to light her candle, she left her script on her seat. As she was reciting her lines in front of a couple of hundred or so of her classmates, teachers, and family, she forgot one word. There was silence. And silence. She just stared to the front trying to conjure up that word. Finally, a teacher took a script up to her and she finished her lines.

She was not willing to do much public speaking the next couple of years after that, until her high school graduation. In front of several hundred of her classmates, teachers and family, she was set to give a valedictorian speech. She prepared well, but I flashed back to her eighth-grade candle-lighting experience. She had matured over the years, but it was still a little unnerving for me. I kept remembering that moment five years earlier when there was nothing I could do but watch my little girl struggle. I would have done anything to have been up there with cue cards for her valedictorian speech, but that was not my *role*. I could not Execute for my daughter.

As it turned out, she was brilliant. She channeled her mom, who speaks in front of crowds of thousands of people. And when I confessed afterward that I had flashed back to the eighth grade, she flawlessly recited her lines from that night long ago. It takes restraint, and often some courage, to let your team just execute. It is like watching your child perform. It is about knowing your role, and its limits.

The Leader and the Execute Phase

The Execute Phase is the time for the leader to *observe and document* if they can. In the Execute Phase, you are relying mainly on your actions in the Leader's Zone to impact performance. If you become a hands-on problem solver, then you risk spending most of your time being what one of my previous managers called a *fireman*—that person who's always putting out fires. This is not an effective or efficient use of a leader's time and energy.

There is another chapter to my story regarding Sarah. She had an experience before her valedictorian speech that totally baffled Linda and me. Even though she was not particularly outgoing in high school and normally avoided situations that called attention to herself, she would occasionally surprise us and put herself out there by trying something new. Most parents feel both excitement and anxiety watching their child playing sports or performing in front of an audience.

However, when Sarah informed her mom and me that she had a solo rap bit in the school talent show her senior year, I had a significantly higher level of anxiety than excitement. I knew that what I could do before her performance was watch her practice and give feedback, encourage her, and help her manage the time she needed to make for practice with the group. But when performance time came, I also knew it was all up to her. We filed into the auditorium, took our seats and watched the acts perform. Then, before I was prepared, Sarah's group took the stage and began their act. There were a handful of girls in the group with a solo bit, and I waited anxiously for Sarah's part. Suddenly, there she was, in front of the group, with the microphone.

I had not seen Sarah in front of a crowd in a personal, vulnerable moment since middle school. I knew there was nothing I could do at that moment to help her, but of course, as her parent, I was totally invested in her success. I wanted her to experience that feeling of success that comes from shining in front of her peers. I will get back to Sarah here in a moment, but I want to stress that leaders should feel very much the same way; you want to invest in your team and be emotionally tied to their success. This is driven by serving as a leader—the notion that you care for your team as people, as well as a means to production.

You lead and prepare people for moments where they take action. Good leaders take full responsibility for their part in preparation, while team members must take full responsibility for their own execution. The leader and the team member both have to take appropriate actions in their roles to succeed. This all comes out in the Debrief Phase.

How invested are you in your people? How important is it to you that your people do a great job the first time—every time—as much for their sake as for the sake of the team? When you are diligent in Focus and tireless in Equip, you set your team up for success. Though I mentioned this before, it's critical to reiterate: Linda's business was not transformed until she focused on the *success* of the *people* on her team.

Leaders in traditional companies sometimes don't appreciate how critical it is to invest in each of their members. You are often conditioned in the corporate world to rank or rate members of your team, but leaders are not driven to make sure **every** member is successful. You just hope for the best, then praise the successful ones and admonish the poorer performers. *Think of the difference focusing on the success of every member would make to your team.*

As I worked with Linda, her organization ballooned into thousands of people with more than fifty top leaders. It became beneficial for Linda to dedicate much of her time to the Focus and Equip Phases. She spent a lot of time on the phone coaching and on the road training. She did not have time to do as much of the fundamental work she had done to build her business originally. We analyzed this carefully and realized that given her skills, talents, timing, and needs of her team, her role in the Leader's Zone for a time was worth the effort, even though it left less time to grow her personal business.

A problem crept in when she found it harder to demonstrate to her team the effort she was putting in. Leadership is a job in itself with its own tasks and Execute Phase, and, especially with smaller or growing companies, it can be difficult to separate leadership activities from day-to-day operations. At the right time, and sometimes for just a period of time, leaders may need to remove themselves from day-to-day responsibilities in operations, making it even more critical that they work the FEED Leader process. When Linda was working side by side with her team, they fed off each other and there was a lot of excitement and energy. Leaders sometimes miss that daily excitement and camaraderie; however, they can still generate and demonstrate that energy and bond by serving their team with vigor.

There are a few points to summarize here. The main actions around the Execute Phase are to observe and document where you can. In support of the Execute Phase, leaders should focus on three areas:

1. In the Equip Phase, invest in your team to a point where you have an emotional stake in every member's success while they are in the Execute Phase.
2. Stress the importance for every member to take responsibility for all of their actions all of the time, while you are responsible for your actions in the Leader's Zone.
3. Always demonstrate your effort and commitment by serving your team, especially if you are no longer involved in the same day-to-day activities they are.

Oh, by the way, Sarah nailed her solo bit in the performance! All the girls did great, but I think she might have been the most notable because everybody who knew Sarah well was in total shock. Rapping lends itself to an aggressive, angry style of delivery unbefitting Sarah's personality, but she reached inside and delivered. A boy approached her after the show and told her he was scared of her now, coming out of her shell like that. Some of her teachers were literally speechless. Some of our friends said they convinced themselves it wasn't really her because they could not believe what they were seeing. As there is pride in a dad seeing his daughter take a risk and succeed, so there is pride in a leader seeing their team execute at a high level.

Summarizing FEED

We have spent a lot of time discussing the value of FEED Leader and dissecting its use as a leadership process. It might be a lengthy process for planning a major initiative, and/or a process you use daily. Just as the work you do in the Focus Phase may apply to several different scenarios you use in the Equip or Debrief Phase, FEED Leader used daily may involve various situations and phases to meet multiple objectives. The important thing is to know what Phase you are in at any moment.

You should also use FEED Leader in cases where you need to make quick decisions and actions. Starting with Focus Phase, you don't always need to recreate work from that phase; just refer to it. Go to Focus first to compare a situation to your overarching plans and design a strategy for the situation. Then to Equip to provide resources and information required. Then to Execute for action, and finally to Debrief to help understand what happened and the consequences that will ensue.

As a leader, there is a lot to manage, but if you remain aware of what Phase you are in at any moment, it can help you understand your role and actions in that situation. When you first start using FEED Leader it might feel awkward, like learning a new language in a foreign country. In learning a language, you might have to stop and think of the English phrase or word and convert it in your head. With FEED Leader, at first you will have to stop and think: "what Phase should I be in for this situation?" Then you think: "what role should I take?"

This is good because you're learning to lead—not with knee-jerk reactions and not solely based on charisma, intelligence, or your personality—but with a process that helps you make consistent, appropriate decisions for any situation. In time, you will become more fluent, and those on your team will see you as a leader who seems to know just what to do in every situation.

We've heard of "natural leaders" whom people are inherently drawn to, or "quiet leaders" who ready their teams with their insight or expertise. But such leadership tends to be limited. When I look for leadership, I don't just seek charisma or intelligence. I want to find the person who knows their role in any circumstance and takes action, someone who is continually leading their team to success. This leader understands the leadership process. You can be that leader, and you can *teach* that kind of leadership. Follow FEED Leader and you will continually reveal the leader within you.

One last thought:

Leaders lead in the Leadership Zone while a team is in operations in the Execute Phase. Understand your role in the Focus, Equip, and Debrief Phases. Your team is dependent on you being a leader. Try FEED Leader diligently for a week. When you are in a leadership moment, think Focus Phase first then move through FEED Leader process and see if it doesn't help you understand actions you need to take.

Notes and Insights:

_____

_____

_____

_____

_____

_____

_____

_____

_____

_____

_____

_____

_____

_____

_____

_____

_____

_____

_____

_____

_____

_____

_____

_____

_____

_____

_____

_____

SECTION III: THE LEADER LEGACY

The Leader Legacy: Building cultural equity from your leadership that can be spread throughout the organization and passed down to other leaders.

CHAPTER 12:
SPREADING INFLUENCE

THERE IS A POINT WHERE your leadership has a residual effect on the organization. You are there even when you are not there. The FEED Leader process helps you ensure that both individuals and leaders on your team are operating well and responding to your leadership. During this process, members of your team see you acting like a leader, and you see how your leaders are leading their teams. However, when you are leading an organization made up of teams it is important to get to a point where your influence is felt when you are not necessarily seen actively leading.

FEED Leader starts this by setting a *climate* to help spread your influence through the organization's *culture*. Think of climate as what you have direct control of and culture is what grows organically. Are you influencing a movement, cause, or revolution people want to join? People will feel that in your culture.

It was critical as her organization grew that Linda had solidified her personal story, her clarity, and her belief, because these elements now belonged to the overall organization. While leaders on your team will eventually develop their own story, clarity, and beliefs for their teams, these qualities should align with those of the organization. Consistency is paramount as things get significantly more complex and you start thinking about leading an organization with leaders and their teams. Working with a small team allows you to manage each individual; however, as your team grows, your actions or decisions will resonate throughout without your direct contact.

Losing Control, Gaining Influence

I worked with a leader who was taking their organization through a transition phase and growth plan. I soon realized that their organizational structure was nebulous and that they had limited procedures and processes. While the leadership wanted to expand the company, they also resisted losing full control of every detail. The more the organization was undefined, the more in control they felt, because employees were forced to go to them for every decision. To get things done in a timely manner, employees adopted the policy of proceeding and letting the leadership correct it later if they didn't like it.

There must be a tradeoff when an organization grows: as leaders share authority, they lose autonomy—but they gain influence. Your teams must understand the organization-wide story, clarity in the vision, and belief as you empower new leaders to do their work. At this point, you should learn to lead through a team of leaders and have less of a direct impact on the individuals in the organization. This means that you need to support your leadership team's decisions.

To that end, when you speak to the entire organization, you may not be privy to specific nuances of how your leaders lead and communicate to their teams. When you do interact with the organization, you need to prepare what you are going to say, speak clearly but broadly, and act consistent with the messages you have shared with your team of leaders.

Some leaders find it hard to work through their team of leaders. They have a strong urge to supplant their leadership team and manage at an individual level. Referring to FEED Leader, leaders need to let their leadership team act in their Execute Phase. If you find yourself with these urges, try to understand what is driving them. Is it a matter of ego? Is it desire to be a problem solver? Do you have trust issues? Do you miss the interaction with the front-line workers? Realize that your work with your leaders is in the Equip and Debrief Phases and that is where you have the most influence.

Focus on using discretion when working with individuals in your organization. I will hear people in Linda's organization advising leaders who are struggling with stagnation in their organizations "to get out of your own way." For your own organization to grow and flourish, you need to get out of the way and let your leaders lead.

To drill down a bit further, members of organizations can have confusion or frustration due to mixed messages from their senior leadership. Some leaders talk indiscriminately: "we may be adding (or cutting) positions or products," or "we may be changing responsibilities within departments." Statements like these can make employees wonder whether their current work is significant.

Other times, the confusion comes from senior leadership asking a member of the organization under someone else's authority to look into something or work on a project. This undermines the direct leader's authority that you gave them in the first place and can decrease productivity. While it's certainly the right of senior leadership or a company owner, this action needs to be handled with discernment. The emphasis here is to be careful how you as a leader interact with members of your organization.

When I coach on the need for leaders to spread influence, I emphasize two areas that leaders need to consider when managing at the organizational level: hierarchy and listening. Both have to do with understanding the organization and how it works. The first is to make sure there is a *clear hierarchy* in leadership. Even in Linda's business, where everyone is an independent representative, there is a place where individuals should go first for advice and direction.

If the idea of having a clearly defined organization under you makes you uncomfortable, it might be a sign that you feel the need for everything to go through you first, which will limit both your own and your organization's growth. There is also a movement in some circles for "open management," or a "flat organization," and removing the "boss" from the organization. I have seen some organizations effectively employ a loose organizational structure; however, in all cases, everyone needs to understand what their role is, even if it is dynamic. And if it is a case where roles change, there must be clear communication every time this happens.

An organization actually has more flexibility and agility with a well-defined organizational structure than with an ambiguous structure. Most people are familiar enough with chess to understand that each piece on the board has a name with specific functions. The skill of the chess player is to maneuver each piece to execute a strategy the best way possible based on the title and roles of the piece. If you don't understand the different pieces' roles, you won't get far with your strategy. Suppose you wanted to be really creative and not follow the rules of chess at all. You would still need to redefine the pieces and their functions for whatever new game you are playing, else there would be chaos. It's hard to be flexible as an organization if you are not clear how things are organized and what can be changed.

The second thing leaders must consider when leading an organization is to designate themselves as the CLO: Chief Listening Officer. You can benefit from having relationships within your organization, being approachable, or having an open door policy. However, it's important to limit relationships with those who are not in your direct team to listening and understanding, and to consistently refer them back to their direct leadership for action. In some situations, a leader may advise someone to go to another leader for specific advice, coaching or mentorship, or advise some intervention; but in any scenario, direct leadership needs to be involved.

Listening to and understanding feelings conveys a lot more power than solving the problems of individuals in most cases. With this understanding, you make an organizational impact in the Focus Phase and Equip Phase. A leader's influence and authority come from setting a climate and culture that empowers people to resolve problems. Your understanding of your organization can give you insight into appropriate climate adjustments. At the same time, listening and understanding helps you understand how well you're leading consistent with a corporate clarity and belief.

Aligning Personal Needs with Organizational Needs

Organizations are intriguing entities no matter their size or structure. They encompass individuals' personal needs and the organization's production needs—rarely with a natural emotional integration between the two. To help with this contrast, you need a purposeful culture. Developing an organization's *culture* is like developing a person's *personality*. You need to find a way to integrate the two.

This can be addressed by looking a little further into climate and culture of an organization. There is another way to distinguish between the climate set and the culture. Good leaders will create a productive climate in which individuals can thrive. We can do this with FEED Leader. Good leaders also nurture a culture in which the collective entity can thrive. *The difference between the two is that in the climate, the leader sets expectations and practices for individual behavior, whereas in the culture, individual behavior sets the expectations and practices for the organization.*

It is easier to align the needs of individuals with the organization if the individuals feel they are contributing to a genuine culture. That means they see consistency in behavior throughout, especially from leadership.

Boss, Manager, and Leader

There is a significant difference between being a boss, managing, and leading when it comes to establishing an organization's culture. A boss controls how people react; managers supervise how people behave; but leaders affect what people *believe*. If you can align your people's beliefs, they will react and behave consistently with your desired culture. Each of these roles is necessary, and leaders need to tackle all three at different times and in different situations. However, when it comes to shaping the organization's culture, *leading* provides the most influence and control.

> *A boss controls how people react; managers supervise how people behave; but leaders affect what people believe.*

It's always important to know who the "boss" is—the person with explicit authority in a situation. It's necessary to play the role of Boss at times, but it's also valuable to limit how much team members perceive their leader as "boss," especially when it comes to developing culture. There have been times in Linda's organization where I've seen someone earn a title based on their performance only to become predominantly a boss. In other words, they started to care more about their position than the people they were leading. This is the trap of "position authority," when it becomes easy to lean on the authority you have because of your title. But if the people following you see you as more of a boss than a leader, they're apt to seek out other leaders to join.

I look at managing as more of an administrative role. When I was in the corporate world, I took a management position. In discussion with a colleague at one point about several areas I felt could be improved regarding my team's operations, I told him I anticipated some great outcomes. As I wrapped up, he told me that if I really wanted to impress our manager, I needed to just make sure my paperwork was timely and accurate, and that my team stayed in line. I was deflated to hear that **my** manager was more interested in managing than leading for success. Sure enough, recognition and rewards went to those who were the best administrators, and not necessarily those whose teams had the best outcomes. Responsible administration has a critical role, but it is not the catalyst for a successful culture.

A leader develops a culture for his or her organization that extends their influence over the entire organization. Even the members of the organization who don't know you well will know your vision, your beliefs, and your expectations. These emanate from direct leaders, processes, and tenured members in addition to what members observe you say and do. A leader's influence is directly correlated with consistency between organizational principles and personal integrity. This kind of organizational influence makes it much easier to share authority and grant autonomy to your leadership team.

One last thought:

Leading is not the same as problem solving. Your influence is felt when your team and organization understand how you want them to act and solve problems. FEED Leader is more of a cause and effect to impact the climate of your team. You also want to have influence, which impacts the culture of your team. How does your team instinctively act and solve problems when you are not around? Does your leadership team instill the same culture you instill in the organization?

Notes and Insights:

_____

_____

_____

_____

_____

_____

_____

_____

_____

_____

_____

_____

_____

_____

_____

_____

_____

_____

_____

_____

_____

_____

_____

_____

_____

_____

_____

Chapter 13:
Epic Leadership

ANYTIME YOU'RE IN ANY GROUP where you motivate and empower others to be productive, you are leading. So, everything I've been talking about here applies to almost anyone. Perhaps you're the CEO of a large company, a parent, a teacher, or a small business owner. Or you might lead a committee at your church or be an officer in a non-profit. Most of us are involved in *some* type of leadership. This is critical to keep in mind as you consider how you can truly make an impact on your organization by developing a culture of success— regardless of what you produce or how big your organization is.

Some leaders who manage a small organization or department might not see themselves as having a leadership team. But if you lead, you have a leadership team. The most efficient thing you can do for your organization is develop leaders. A parent with a spouse and two kids can have a leadership team. Perhaps the older sibling helps lead when it comes to the younger sibling.

You may not have an "official" team of leaders if you manage a small department at work, but you know who your leaders are. Whether it's formal or informal, *your team of leaders comprises those you depend on to share the vision with others throughout the organization.* Whether these people have recognized titles or not, it's crucial to encourage them to lead.

Build a Consistent Culture

When I started to put together ideas for how I could help others find success as leaders based on the principles that have brought Linda and me success for well over a decade, I turned to the element at the core of that success: the culture. Linda's organization consists of independent business people. However, the methods and messages have to be consistent to maintain the desired culture. From time to time, there may be different methods and messages from outside her organization that influence some members of her organization. Linda will support these individuals the best she can, but they have a hard time fitting into the culture of her organization, which can be disruptive.

Corporate organizations could benefit from understanding this. There can be several "good" ways to do something, but things run more efficiently when leadership decides upon one method, climate, and culture, and sticks with it. Things can fall apart rapidly in companies where employees aren't sure how to act, react, or behave because of inconsistent signals from leadership. This can stunt an organization's growth.

Linda recognizes this. She explains to her team that it is like you are on Diet A and someone else is on Diet B. Both are good diets, but the dinner menu is going to be Diet A in our organization, and someone on Diet B might not have a lot of selection. If you mix the diets, you won't get the desired results. Of course, the worst-case scenario is if the leadership wants the organization to be on Diet A and the leaders are feasting on anything they want.

Culture of Success

With the race-car driver analogy, we discussed how some drivers are known as champions and everyone associated with them is part of a Culture of Success. Developing a Culture of Success depends on how you influence the core of your organization to where there is existential clarity—that is, clarity on why the organization exist. It means asking: how do we grow this culture to where it instinctively and consistently finds success? How do we maintain the culture so it is resistant to forces that tend to corrode an organization?

Let's compare two types of cultures: one where success is inconsistent and one where success is an inherent expectation. In some groups, for some reason, things sometimes work out, and sometimes they don't. Maybe a competitor often seems to get the best clients, or some years they grow and other years they don't. They never seem to consistently be on top of things. In contrast, other groups find that no matter how dire the situation, they always know that they are going to be successful. They feel it is inconceivable that they could fail if they have worked hard and have done what they were supposed to do.

Have you ever felt that way ... that you just couldn't lose? Perhaps a sports team you're a fan of was on an extremely successful streak. Even when they were down, you knew they would find a way to make it. There were disappointments, but the disappointments were huge growth moments that propelled the team to even more success. Maybe you work for an organization that always seems to be the top performer in its industry. This is how our last fourteen-plus years have felt in our business. And this is the state I want to help other leaders reach.

I recognized that thriving organizations develop a Culture of Success because they have an extremely high sense of awareness. Part of this comes from the anticipation we talked about in the Action part of CBA, but at an organizational level. Leaders and their organizations take action and anticipate opportunities. They know where they are going and what they are doing. They have a clear idea of how they need to act, and they have confidence in their skills and abilities to produce.

How would you feel if you worked in an organization that was highly motivated and had people with good character who were very good at what they did? Now, imagine if leadership treated *everyone* that way. How could an organization like that *not* thrive?

I want to introduce a paradigm I designed from my observations and experience. I created this paradigm to emphasize and integrate these principles for leaders, and to enable them to develop and maintain a Culture of Success. Sometimes a combination of principles or concepts is referred to as a "construct." I call this the **EPIC Construct,** because it shows what happens when you integrate the concepts of Excellence in **P**urpose, in **I**ntegrity, and in **C**apacity:

EPIC Construct – The intentional effort to continually develop Excellence in Purpose, Integrity, and Capacity results in a Culture of Success.

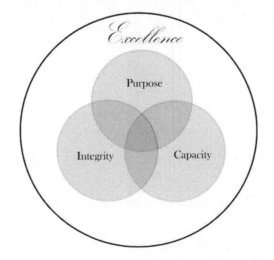

The diagram highlights critical areas where the concepts for developing a Culture of Success overlap. These areas of strength are where you start to see the culture coalesce and thrive, and where its leaders can say the following:

- **Purpose + Integrity:** *Not only are the people in my organization highly motivated by a strong purpose; they also have strong character.* Strength in this area prevents corrosion of the culture from vulnerabilities from lack of motivation or weak character.

- **Capacity + Purpose:** *The people in my organization are great at what they do and are highly motivated.* Strength in this area is the quality production that sets the organization apart from others.

- **Integrity + Capacity:** *My people have strong character and are great at what they do.* This strength here highlights the organization's efficiency due to highly competent people who act with good judgment.

If this seems familiar, it's because it is related to our experience with personal development when we focused on Personal Character, Personal Fulfillment and Personal Achievements. These are similar concepts to EPIC, but there is a different approach based on the dynamics of working with an organization where you can't directly control behavior. You need a Culture of Success.

The "Triple A" Leader

Before we explore this construct further, I want to emphasize how important it is to be what I call a "Triple A" Leader when implementing EPIC Leadership. The three A's are the qualities of

Awareness, Anticipation, and Accountability that leaders must possess to cultivate each area: Purpose, Integrity, and Capacity.

At Merck, I was introduced to an analysis process that is a very practical way to think about Awareness, Anticipation, and Accountability. Many of you might be familiar with this approach— or some variation of it—called S.W.O.T. analysis. Envision a square with four quadrants labeled from the top row left to right: Strengths, Weaknesses, Opportunities, and Threats. This is a great exercise to do routinely to test the culture of the organization.

In the left two quadrants you list things you want to grow and leverage. You highlight your organization's *internal* Strengths and *external* Opportunities. In the right two quadrants you list the things you need to shore up or minimize: your *internal* Weaknesses and *external* Threats.

Strengths (Internal)	Weaknesses (Internal)
Opportunities (External)	Threats (External)

When I use the S.W.O.T. analysis to work with leaders, I challenge them to survey their teams to validate the results before we go on to develop strategies. I've seen managers put a lot of energy into designing strategies after a S.W.O.T. session, only to realize that their premise did not resonate throughout the organization. While leadership always has the final say, it benefits everyone to periodically test your thoughts within the organization. Once you've completed this analysis and have focused on your organization's general culture, you are more *Aware*, know what to *Anticipate*, and realize where you need to have *Accountability*. By the way, using FEED to implement EPIC, you would be in the Focus Phase at this point.

When I talked earlier about developing your story, I touched on the dynamics time can play here—and to be aware of where you are in your story. One of the hardest things to explain to a leader who is struggling with consistency is their need to remain *Aware* of where they are, what they are doing, and how things have changed. There's a reason Awareness is the first "A" in Triple A Leadership; it is critical to know what is going on in your surroundings, within your organization, and most importantly, how circumstances might have changed. You need to stay engaged and be attentive, or it will be difficult to implement a Culture of Success.

We've already discussed the second "A," Anticipation, regarding the *personal* activities required for personal growth. Anticipation in relation to the Triple A Leader is more focused on anticipation of actions beyond your control. The concept is the same, though: with an action from any source you should anticipate a result. Be aware of the actions going on around you and anticipate results from that action, even if it is a long time coming. This is a proactive, forward-looking posture that helps the organization understand where it is headed and what to expect along the way. It also calls for the leader to consider contingencies. Even when things do not go as originally planned, a leader must still guide the organization with a planned alternative.

The third "A" is Accountability. Starting with leadership and moving throughout the organization, you must focus on accountability to develop a Culture of Success. In EPIC Leadership, leaders must first commit to abide by the strategies and standards set in developing and implementing Purpose, in instilling Integrity, and in building Capacity throughout the organization.

Focus on Behavior

Leadership must also commit to recognizing and rewarding behaviors that members of the organization demonstrate. Professional sales teams are very good at this. When I worked as a field representative for Merck, it didn't take me long to realize which behaviors would make management recognize and reward me. Even though they weren't specifically using the EPIC Construct, I can see upon looking back how different recognitions could be segmented into Purpose, Integrity, and Capacity.

Even though management did a great job of recognizing my *outcomes* at Merck, they put just as much—and possibly more— emphasis on recognizing *behavior*, and it was very impactful. Importantly, accountability was almost always reinforced with positive acknowledgement. When I moved into management, I learned the significance of the mantra of public recognition and private admonishment. Even so, most people on our team worked for the recognition, and admonishment was a rare event.

If you continually focus on behavior of Excellence in Purpose, Integrity, and Capacity, you will notice the people who you lead doing the same. A leader who is focused on EPIC can feel when things are running smoothly or when there is something wrong under the hood. They can use the FEED Leader process to maintain or correct operations when appropriate. However, the further down the road you are with EPIC, the more you will notice self-maintenance and self-correction—which allows you more time to spend on progress and vision.

As we move into a deeper discussion of EPIC, I want you to keep in mind the **EPIC Rule** for building a Culture of Success: *In an effort to pursue excellence in any of the three principles, Purpose, Integrity, or Capacity, if you diminish excellence in any principle in order to expand excellence in another principle you will weaken the Culture of Success.* It helps to understand this as you study the Attributes for Purpose, Integrity, and Capacity listed at the end of the next three chapters.

For example, if you hire someone who takes *initiative* and is *persistent* to increase Capacity, but you did not consider that this same person will likely reduce *morale* in Purpose or *restraint* in Integrity, then the hire can ultimately have a negative effect on the Culture of Success. As decisions are made and actions taken, consider the impact on expanding excellence in each principle—Purpose, Integrity and Capacity. There needs to be an effort to continually and simultaneously expand excellence in all three principles.

Decision or Action	
Excellence in Purpose	✔
Excellence in Integrity	✔
Excellence in Capacity	✔

One last thought:
A Culture of Success is about winning. Unless you are in a sports organization, it is not common to think about your organization "winning." The cumulative effect of Excellence in Purpose, Integrity and Capacity placed in the context of winning can give your organization a competitive drive. Notice the leaders in your life and what they do to promote Purpose, Integrity, and Capacity.

Notes and Insights:

_____

_____

_____

_____

_____

_____

_____

_____

_____

_____

_____

_____

_____

_____

_____

_____

_____

_____

_____

_____

_____

_____

_____

_____

_____

CHAPTER 14:
EXCELLENCE IN PURPOSE

DEVELOPING EXCELLENCE IN PURPOSE IS personal to me, largely because it reminds me of the hardship I endured as a 29-year-old husband with a new born and feeling no hope for financial security. I still get panic attacks whenever my family or company faces any kind of financial hiccup. I mentioned earlier that I needed to find the faith that God was going to ultimately provide, whatever that looked like. Thanks to my loving wife, family, good friends, and a supportive church family, I found that faith—and it filled me with hope that provided the energy I needed to press on.

When I think about purpose, I correlate it to my Christian faith. Sometimes faith is a strange thing. The less I perceive I need it, the easier it is to feel like I have it. But the more I feel I need it, the harder it is to embrace. Then there are those times where faith is all I have left. I believe God allows me to have those panic attacks to remind me how I felt when I finally, genuinely admitted to myself that I wasn't going to fix things on my own, and that He was totally in charge. Of course, faith should carry me through both good times and bad. Thanks to my bad times, I realized my purpose: to glorify God, and let Him work through me to help others find success. I would like all people to know Christ, but my mission is to help people find success in their lives and their business regardless of their faith—and hope that they will see Christ in me in the process.

As with faith, it is sometimes hard to realize how strong our purpose is when things are going well or when we are just cruising on auto-pilot. *But, with a strong purpose, the good times are more meaningful, and the times of crisis are more focused.*

Aligning Organizational Purpose with Personal Purpose

My purpose is not just the words put down in a mission or vision statement; it is a *feeling* driven by desires and beliefs. It is important to understand this, because *everyone* has a purpose, whether they can articulate it or not. The challenge as a leader is finding and promoting a purpose for your organization and, importantly, aligning that purpose with each of its members.

When Linda was initially trying to grow her business, her purpose was to find people to help her be successful. But she was not attracting the type of people she needed, since very few could align *their* personal purpose with trying to make Linda successful. When she realized her purpose was in fact to serve others and help *them* succeed, she started attracting people who could align their own ambitions with the organization's goals and trajectory. No wonder that some of those successful leaders on her team are/were doctors, teachers, nurses, therapists, moms, public service employees, and others with a heart to serve.

Most organizations do, and all organizations *should*, have a **documented** mission or vision statement. As leaders, it's crucial that we understand the organizational purpose behind that vision statement. At Merck, we believed that we made the best products and that our products helped save lives and improved quality of life. We learned the science behind why we should feel that way; but more importantly, we were constantly reminded of the personal stories from people who were affected by the diseases we were trying to prevent. Hearing those stories firsthand made it easy to feel good about our purpose; most people can align their purpose with saving lives.

We didn't just talk about it; our leadership at Merck was committed to it. As representatives, we built our messages around the science and quality—not what we could give our customers. There are many tales of big, bad pharmaceutical companies out there. That is not what I experienced with Merck. We were not allowed to take doctors golfing, take them on trips, or provide many perks at all. Our focus was on educating and communicating the value of our products.

I called on one influential doctor every month who was always difficult to get time with. His office was about sixty miles away, on the outskirts of my territory. Whenever I got an opportunity to talk to him, we delved into medical studies regarding the science of our business. When I arrived there one afternoon, I waited for at least an hour, then was informed that he was not going to be available that afternoon. I decided to get a hotel room that night and try to talk to him the next morning. The morning went something like this:

"Good morning Stacey, I'm here to see Dr. Smith. Can I grab a few minutes with him?" I asked the nurse when I arrived.

"I'm so sorry Joel, he is overbooked this morning and he's going to be out of the office this afternoon. He just isn't going to have time," the nurse said before she turned to put patients' charts on the doors.

Just then, Dr. Smith (not his actual name) came out of a patient's room and saw me at the nurse's station. He said something to the nurse and proceeded into the next room to see his next patient. Nurse Stacey headed back to the nurse's station where I was standing.

"The doctor wants you to come and wait in his office," Stacey said as she motioned me to follow her. "Are you sponsoring Dr. Smith for a symposium at a beach resort or something?" she asked almost sarcastically.

"No, I just want to discuss the study I left with him last time," I answered. "I don't have any programs like that to offer him."

I waited in his office for at least another hour before he made it in.

"Hi, Joel, the only reason I'm meeting you in my office is that you come by every month and you always have something substantive to talk about. I enjoy discussing the studies you bring by," Dr. Smith explained.

As I left his office half an hour later, Stacey caught me and told me that he never meets reps in his office. She wondered what was so important that I had to share. I told her we just reviewed a study. Merck's emphasis on our purpose for our division reflected in my behavior, and our customers noticed.

We've already discussed the importance of personal growth in leading others, and the necessity of finding clarity through developing our story and building our belief. I use the equation that Clarity + Belief = Purpose to illustrate this point. *(Not to get too deep into the algebra of this, but if Clarity + Belief = Purpose and if, as discussed when we talked about CBA, Clarity fills Belief and Belief fuels Action, then it makes sense that Purpose (Clarity + Belief) fuels Action - What do you think?)* In essence, understanding what is important to us, combined with belief in ourselves and our goals, is our purpose. It's nearly impossible to develop a purpose for an organization without having a personal purpose in mind, since the organization's purpose needs to be an extension of its leader's purpose. Don't neglect purpose.

One of a leader's important roles is to help make the purpose real for their team. When I am training groups on EPIC Leadership, I explain the process:

1. Leaders **establish** purpose.
2. Leaders **share their vision** for purpose.
3. Members of the organization **embrace belief** in that purpose.
4. Finally, members of the organization **act** with purpose.

Leaders integrate their people into the organizational purpose. Leaders help their people find clarity and build belief in themselves and the organizational purpose.

Notice also how this is established in the four FEED Leader Phases: in the Focus Phase to establish purpose, in the Equip Phase to share the purpose, and in the Execute Phase when the organization embraces and acts with purpose. From there, use the Debrief Phase to assess the consistency and reward behavior.

I read an article in *Fortune* magazine several years ago that really struck me. Mars, Inc., puts a lot of value in their employees, or "associates," as they call them. It is a private, family-owned company but with brands just as segmented as any publicly held conglomerate. The *Fortune* article stated that Mars doesn't believe they serve their customers well by offering trendy benefits like private chefs, Foosball tables, or luxurious office buildings for their employees; rather, they pride themselves in building camaraderie and cultivating opportunities for their employees. They **established purpose** in showing employees they are part of a community and encouraging them to thrive in this community. They also show their employees the value they want to offer the customer.

Across all their brands, Mars **shares the vision of their purpose** as they reinforce the Five Principles of quality, responsibility, mutuality, efficiency, and freedom. Throughout 73 countries and 400 offices, regardless of brand, these Five Principles are displayed, emphasized, and are a standard of behavior towards each other and their community. So as employees are encouraged to expand their careers by crossing brands and countries, they remain part of the same Mars community.

The company reinforces this purpose as they create opportunities for employees to serve in their communities and around the world. The employees **embrace belief** in this purpose as they see the company willing to invest in them. Within this purpose, the company is staunchly opposed to going public. Management doesn't have to work under the confines of investor expectations as a private company. Employees are encouraged to explore and experiment often as **they act with purpose**, which fosters innovation and loyalty.

Finding Purpose

Purpose is the reason you move; it is the fuel for your fire, the energy for your motion. (We just suggested above that Purpose fuels Action.) If you want to drive action to success, there needs to be clarity and belief behind any action the organization requires. And to help develop clarity, you must develop the organization's story just as you did for personal growth. You need to work closely with your teams to guide individuals in creating *their* stories and align them with the organization's story.

> *Purpose is the reason you move; it is the fuel for your fire, the energy for your motion.*

Early in this book I distinguished joining a leader from following a leader. People join a movement, cause, or revolution. What is important about thinking of your organization in these terms is that they represent change or progress. Not in a combative or radical sense, but in the sense that people feel like what they do can move the bar on something that is important to them. You might be thinking - it is going to be hard to get my team to rally around manufacturing toilet paper or distributing nuts and bolts or whatever your core business is. You may be right, if the only reason to be in business was to make money.

Beyond generating revenue, consider these questions:

Why does my organization exist?

_____

_____

_____

_____

What makes being part of my organization so special to its members?

_____

_____

_____

_____

What do I want external stakeholders to say about my organization?

_____

_____

_____

_____

Which of my organizational standards will not be compromised under any circumstance, regardless how it affects the bottom line?

_____

_____

_____

_____

I remember being involved in a discussion with a group that included members from the corporate office of the company that produces the products that Linda sells. They had recently discontinued a product that was very popular, and the independent representatives were trying to see if there was any way corporate could get this product back on the market. The problem was that certain components of the product were not available anymore, and the substitute components did not meet the standards of the company. There was lost revenue in that decision, but there was significant "purpose capital" gained.

Your team will be motivated when their work represents something they believe in at an organizational and personal level. This is where you find the most significant distinction between the boss, manager, and leader. The leader exhibits patience, understanding, and willingness to support team members as they develop. Employees then begin to work and think with more purpose and motivation. Again, start with the organization's and leader's beliefs as benchmarks for individual beliefs. Teach the same CBA principles you used for personal growth.

Some organizations I have been associated with use an effective method for creating positive cultural change. The idea is to focus on a word or concept over time. Members adopt that word, and it becomes a trigger of sorts to adjust their behavior during the routine of their lives.

A lot of you have been doing this for a long time to help you adjust a behavior, possibly without being aware of it. Have you ever written a word on a mirror or a place of prominence to remind you how you want to think or act? A football team might have a sign in their locker room that says, "Never Quit!" Some of you might focus on a word like "Perseverance" or "Patience" depending on what you want to improve on. Others of you might put a word on the wall near your phone or a sticky note on the edge of your computer screen where you will see it often. It's a great device to trigger a desired response when the right situation comes up.

To take advantage of this method, I have distributed several words that I call "attributes" into three groups that align with Purpose, Integrity, and Capacity. The idea is to develop a consistent vocabulary and standard of behavior that you can apply throughout an organization. For the Purpose principle of the EPIC Construct, I chose the attributes of Conviction, Dedication, Engagement, Enthusiasm, Influence, Insight, Inspiration, Loyalty, and Motivation. As a leader promoting Purpose, you study, teach, and reinforce these attributes with your organization. For instance, when you tell someone in your organization that you appreciate their Conviction to our Purpose, they and others know exactly what you are saying.

At your next weekly or monthly staff meeting, introduce or emphasize a new attribute. For instance, the description of Enthusiasm *is showing a marked interest and energy in pursuing an initiative.* This meeting would be a good time to teach and apply this attribute by recognizing someone who showed Enthusiasm for the Purpose of the organization. Find a way to focus on each attribute, and you will notice that attribute becoming more apparent in your culture.

Purpose Attributes

Conviction: Establishing a deep belief that does not waver in the face of challenges.

Dedication: Demonstrating commitment by staying engaged and focused even in the face of adversity.

Engagement: Interacting with others with an open and appealing disposition.

Enthusiasm: Showing a marked interest and energy in pursuing an initiative.

Influence: Having a persuasive force that affects a person's actions, beliefs. or behavior.

Insight: Being reflective and thoughtful to understand the true nature of a situation.

Inspiration: Moving others to thoughts or actions beyond expectations or standards.

Loyalty: Faithful commitment to those who have earned and expect it, despite personal repercussions.

Motivation: Moved to take productive actions based on a purpose, reason, or inspiration.

A strong organizational Purpose is an amazingly motivating force. To promote your purpose, you need to do more than write it down somewhere and say it; you need to align it with the purpose of your people. An effective way of doing this is to encourage and reinforce behavior that matches your organization's purpose. Take time to study and teach each attribute, think of ways to align with Purpose, and reinforce these attributes throughout the organization. Help your organization build Excellence in Purpose.

One last thought:

How do you motivate an organization? Give them a purpose to stand behind. Take some time in the Focus Phase of FEED Leader and contemplate what Purpose means to your organization and how you can instill that in the Equip Phase. If you think about it, most motivational speeches you hear are based on driving home a purpose.

Notes and Insights:

Chapter 15:
Excellence in Integrity

THERE IS A DIFFERENCE BETWEEN thinking you have integrity and actually having integrity—the difference being that integrity must be your number one priority all the time. When you merely think you have it, you tend to make your ambition the number one priority and work in integrity where it fits. You want to reverse that: to act with integrity first and foremost, then work in your *ambition* where it fits.

Integrity is your defense, your shield, and your peace; it makes your organization structurally sound. When there is a design dispute between an architect and an engineer, who should win? The engineer should win! It doesn't matter how beautiful the building is if there are cracks, sagging beams, or structural failure.

Leaders Set the Tone for Integrity

Leaders who want to maintain a positive culture for their organization need first to look in the mirror. It is difficult to separate the character of the leader from the integrity of the organization they lead. I have seen multiple definitions for character and integrity. So, to clarify, I am going to generally refer to character as the moral and ethical characteristics that an individual consistently exhibits, and integrity as adherence to a set of moral and ethical standards.

Regardless of what the leader says or what is in the employee manual, his or her character establishes the standards that the organization strives to adhere to.

Linda has many mentors in her business. One of these, a close friend, Cecilia, would tell her to always "assume best intentions" when there was an issue or conflict with others. Cecilia is an integral part of Linda's success and freely shares business advice from her experiences. Now, I consistently hear Linda say the same thing to her team. "Assume best intentions" means that we have a standard of how we behave towards each other, and our first reaction is to act as if that standard is upheld.

It is easier to show good character with a proactive action than with a reaction. Linda takes and encourages this approach because she wants to mitigate the reaction to something that may or may not have actually happened. Usually there is a misunderstanding involved, but even in cases where there isn't, she wants her people to focus on the initial incident when everyone has had time to think and things aren't complicated by knee-jerk reactions.

If there is no standard, then there is no way to measure whether standards were adhered to. Standards have to be set before there can be an assumption that people are adhering to them. So as the organization follows this mantra, the members start to develop characteristics of patience, graciousness, understanding, discretion, and so on. Linda and her leadership team consistently demonstrate these attributes, which help other members of the organization accept and recommunicate this standard throughout.

The leader or leadership group should be the most influential people within your organization when it comes to integrity. You need to reflect on Personal Growth and Leadership Growth, because they are concurrent processes that have reciprocating value. Personal growth helps you understand how to be a good leader, while leadership growth helps you understand ways you need to grow personally.

Excellence in Integrity with CBA and FEED

It's so critical to build an organization with people who consistently show good character that I want to go back to the notions of CBA and FEED Leader (Focus, Equip, Execute, Debrief) to step through this concept. The way people describe you is part of your story. What are the things that shaped you into who you are now? What moral or ethical decisions did you make that define you? I have found in the many gracious leaders who work with Linda—people who lead with a servant's heart and a genuine interest in helping others find success— a behavior that naturally gravitates towards developing good character.

Personal Character is the foundation of personal growth. The processes of creating and telling your story will help you figure out what kind of person you *want* to be and *need* to be to lead others. A large part of this is to identify your own moral and ethical standards and act in accordance with them, whatever the situation. You should also understand why your standards are important and purposefully make decisions that further define your character. Again, a leader cannot effectively instill a set of guidelines for an organization if those guidelines are not consistent with the leader's character.

As a leader, Excellence in Integrity starts in the Focus Phase of FEED Leader as you set the values and principles for the organization. What do you want your members' character and organization's integrity to look like? While a lot of companies train employees on policies and compliance, I'm not sure how many actually have a practical plan for training and reinforcing *integrity*. Leaders must continually grow an environment where integrity goes beyond company compliance.

They need to consider the moral, ethical, industry, organizational, and personal standards in establishing Excellence in Integrity, and do so via proactive, consistent, and continual initiatives. The Focus Phase is the time to establish a process to use in the Debrief Phase to evaluate and reinforce the character of the members and the organization's integrity.

When I decided to set up a company whose purpose was to help strengthen organizations, I wanted the branding to represent something living, dynamic, and strong. I was drawn to the teak tree, because it is one of the strongest and most damage-resistant trees. So, I named my company Teak Leadership Group. While I can draw several analogies between an organization and a teak tree, I want to concentrate here on its internal strength. One thing that makes the teak tree's wood so useful for boats, outdoor furniture, and other highly exposed uses is how well it can withstand adverse conditions. The oils in the teak tree make teak wood water-resistant and protect it from dry rot, fungi, parasites, and insects. I see integrity as these oils running through an organization, keeping it strong, and protecting it from decay and external forces. Because these oils exist, all other functions of the tree work better. Integrity bolsters Purpose and Capacity.

Teak Tree Forest

The Equip Phase for growing Excellence in Integrity is a daily process. You want to think that the people in your organization will make the best decisions. But *leaders* must have made the investment in teaching, training, modeling, and coaching to ensure that happens. Your members should hear consistent messages from everyone on the leadership team when it comes to integrity.

Because of the planning you did in the Focus Phase and the effort you took in the Equip Phase, you will be prepared to take action in the Debrief Phase as your team is in the Execute Phase. There are three segments I look for when evaluating Excellence in Integrity in the Debrief Phase. I segment behavior by *Actions, Reactions,* and *Interactions*.

- *Actions* are what I define as consistent or anticipated behavior. Phrases I hear as a warning sign that are typical of Actions that need attention are "that is the way we have always done it," or "everyone does it that way." When you hear this, you take immediate action to address the situation by moving to the Focus Phase to head off the situation systemically. I find Leaders tend to address these issues in the Debrief Phase but aren't as effective in addressing the issues in the Focus Phase and, subsequently, the Equip Phase. *Actions* that counter principles or values are usually *due to a lack of belief in the principles or values* or lack of respect for the leadership in correcting behavior. It is important to discover the underlying situation in the Debrief Phase and move to the Focus Phase to evaluate how to address the underlying situation

- *Reactions* are isolated, immediate responses to a situation or circumstance. In the Debrief Phase, it is important to distinguish between systemic Actions and isolated Reactions.

It is satisfying to see a team member react in a way consistent with the principles and values you established in the Focus Phase and trained in the Equip Phase. But there are times you need to address unexpected and isolated Reactions that are inconsistent with your principles and values. Whereas undesirable Actions stem from lack of belief, undesirable Reactions stem from *lack of knowledge, understanding, or judgement in regard to principles and values*. Understanding the difference between Actions and Reactions will help a leader use good judgement in addressing a negative situation.

Although it seems inconsistent, the most effective thing to do in some cases is to have a different level of punitive response for the same negative behavior from two different individuals based on whether it is an Action or Reaction. Also, it helps to know in the Equip Phase if you are addressing lack of belief or lack of knowledge or understanding.

I had a summer job when I was in college at a food-manufacturing plant. There was one full-time employee who consistently found opportunities to shirk responsibilities and nap during the workday. On the other hand, a fellow summer worker had a better work ethic, but one afternoon he needed to take care of a personal issue, so he left his post, where he felt he wouldn't be missed. The first employee would be classified as an issue with "Action" in Debrief because he was compelled to challenge integrity. The second employee would be classified as an issue with "Reaction" because he made a bad decision and showed poor judgment. It helps to understand this as you address each individual in the Debrief and Equip Phases.

— *Interactions* are responses due to relationships with others. Someone might have a deep belief in the principles and values in *Actions*, and have a good knowledge, understanding and judgement of the principles and values in *Reactions*, but have difficulties demonstrating those principles and values in *Interactions* with others. Examples include personality conflicts, unhealthy competition, or influences someone holds over another. Recall from our discussions on FEED Leader that Debrief Phase is when you react to what has happened in the Execute Phase, and Equip Phase is when you prepare your team for the Execute Phase. In the Debrief Phase, help your team understand where others have power or influence over them (giving up power is letting anyone alter your behavior by what they say or do OR by what you think they will say or do). In the Equip Phase, you prepare them with confidence and foresight to have positive Interactions.

Consider these questions while engaged in FEED Leader for yourself or towards your team: How do you plan to act when there is an opportunity for personal gain if you compromise integrity and go against your character? How do you react when you're tired or in a hurry to finish some work, and it would be easier to take shortcuts? What do you do when you have an opportunity to assist someone who irritates you? What do you say when it is easier to mislead someone than explain the situation, or when someone is getting under your skin? What do you tell coworkers when you're frustrated with your manager? *It is a matter of defining your behavior through your Actions, Reactions, and Interactions.*

Excellence in Integrity means growing a culture where individuals feel compelled to make decisions based on their belief in underlying standards and principles. It takes effort to Equip for Excellence in

Integrity, because you need to align the organization's beliefs with your standards and principles as you prepare your people to react and interact appropriately in any situation.

The nature of the business Linda is in doesn't require all members to work at a common location on a daily basis. The team is spread across the United States and beyond. Usually, there is a lot of electronic and social media communication, along with routine meetings or occasional trips to different locations. This dynamic makes it especially important to maintain a culture of Excellence in Integrity in her organization; with limited direct contact and little power based on position, members must maintain a strong belief in organizational values and standards. The pressure to act a certain way needs to come more from the culture, not from proximity of leaders and coworkers who enforce rules and regulations. Generally, the more rules you have to put in place, the less influence you have in your organization.

I worked for a manager that taught and reinforced the concept that we should always treat each other with respect. His influence over our team caused us to reinforce this concept with each other. In those times that a member did not treat a teammate with respect, there was considerable pressure from the rest of the team for them to reconsider their action or reaction. It was not necessary for our manager to create a rule for dishonesty towards a teammate, speaking negatively about a teammate, taking credit for someone else's work, or any other manner of showing disrespect because of his influence in our team.

Leadership needs to explicitly demonstrate integrity to its organization. This is why it is important to have character that is consistent with organizational standards. This can be difficult at times, but *consistent and visible acts of integrity at the expense of some personal gain can have a resounding, positive effect throughout an organization.* When a leader turns down a lucrative contract because fulfilling that contract would compromise the organization's principles, then the organization has a model of behavior.

During Debrief Phase, the leadership team needs to reinforce positive behavior. Here we want to acknowledge and reward behavior in planned actions, reactions, and interactions that are consistent with organizational principles. Make the language of the principles part of the vocabulary of the organization. Every once in a while, I hear someone on Linda's team say "assume best intentions," because it is part of their language now. When something like that happens, recognize and appreciate that team member's adherence to the principles.

Developing Individual Character

Growing an organization with integrity at the core of its culture helps develop individuals with exemplary character. It can be difficult to overcome the failure of any one individual with poor character. If an individual in your organization doesn't exhibit a strong belief in your Purpose or a high Capacity to perform, there are usually others who can pick up the slack. But if even one individual shows poor character, it can be at best distracting, and at worst destructive to an organization.

When I owned a construction company, I was talking to a superintendent who had just fired a framing crew. I asked him why he fired this crew and he said it was because they were stealing materials from the job site. This was curious to me because I had worked with the foreman of this crew before and I never had trouble with his crews. I went to talk to this foreman and he told me that, in fact, a member of his crew had taken material off a job site. He said he fired him immediately and replaced the material. This was an appropriate gesture, but he had an issue now with contractors being leery of using his crew.

If this member of his crew was not highly motivated (Purpose) or not being productive (Capacity) that day, I'm sure no one would have noticed as long as the work was being completed to an acceptable standard. However, that member of the crew showed poor Integrity that day and it cost everyone on that crew new jobs.

> *...an optimally functioning team is much more effective than any individual performance.*

You want to grow all three of the concepts of the EPIC Construct in concert, but the leader needs to be especially vigilant in growing Integrity. Ironically, it is often integrity that leaders let slide with employees, especially highly motivated high performers. This is damaging when trying to develop a Culture of Success. Focusing on consistent adherence to the organization's set of principles will give you a platform to nurture individuals with strong character, even when you might be sacrificing productivity at an individual level. Just remember, an optimally functioning team is much more effective than any individual performance.

Those of us who hire know the conflict this can create. You might encounter an outstanding candidate with impressive credentials but notice some red flags when it comes to their character. How tempting is it to think "I can fix them," or "that's just the situation they were in." A great place to start building Excellence in Integrity is in the hiring process. Don't be afraid to weigh character heavily in hiring. It can pay dividends later.

We see this in sports teams where a talented player has some serious character issues. The question is: "should we take a chance on him or her?" You probably know stories where that decision backfired. Consider these scenarios: the top salesperson candidate has some questionable sales techniques. The best candidate for a machine operator job is crude and makes everyone else's day miserable. The most efficient administrative assistant candidate makes inappropriate innuendos. Everyone deserves a second chance, but unless you've spent due diligence with character and you're convinced it has been resolved, don't move forward. If you have to ask yourself if a potential employee is worth the risk because of their character, then generally, they are not.

Excellence in Integrity is an Important Part of Culture

Linda always implores her team to "edify their leaders." Leaders allow individuals and teams to focus on their productivity. Whether you are part of a small or large organization, leaders are there to serve a team, so its members can focus on their tasks. A leader might be handling a myriad of priorities and wearing multiple hats at any given time. This appeal to "edify your leaders" speaks to the fact that we must honor and respect those who have responsibilities and experience and are there to serve their teams—or at least do not diminish their position within the organization.

It is equally important for leaders to edify their teams. Any hint that you are unhappy or displeased with a team member, except to that member alone (or a mentor for advice), hinders that member's growth because it adds a barrier to overcome with others.

An environment with a high standard of integrity—where individuals demonstrate exemplary character—can be a place individuals enjoy being in and where they thrive. As leaders, you have the power to create an environment based on trust, confidence, understanding, loyalty, and support—one where people are more likely to share ideas, take risks, admit mistakes, correct mistakes, put in extra effort, and are easy to work with. An environment like this also tends to have increased retention, even when compensation is modest.

When I train and consult on EPIC, I give a list of tips to leaders to implement personally then share with their teams when they are facing situations that might test their integrity. We usually have everyone role-play these tips among the team. Envision yourself doing this activity as you review the following list, and see if it helps you think about integrity:

- **Continually teach/learn the standards and values:** Just the knowledge and understanding of an organization's values and policies can help you recognize and correct your behavior before you make a bad decision.

- **Serve others:** As leaders, you serve so that others can be productive. When you must question a decision's integrity, it can help to ask how this will help you serve others for the benefit of the organization.

- **Smile before you act or speak:** For most of us, it is uncomfortable to smile when you are acting against your conscience.

- **Clarify before you respond:** Make sure you understand what you are reacting to. You can often react negatively based on a misunderstanding or an emotionally charged moment. If nothing else, this gives you a moment to think before you react or speak.

- **Will someone find out?** If your adrenaline spikes at the thought of anyone ever finding out what you are going to say or do, then consider whether it is something you should be doing at all. Be assured, someone will find out.

- **Think integrity first, reward second:** A series of reward-based decisions can subtly take you down a path that challenges your integrity. Think "is it right?" before you think "will this benefit me?"

- **Look around before you act or speak:** Become aware of your situation. You tend to get "tunnel vision" once you decide to counter your principles or act out of character. Physically looking around and understanding where you are and what you are doing can help you recover perspective.

- **Understand when you are tired or impaired:** When you are tired or impaired for any reason, be mindful that you are more susceptible to poor decision-making. *Exhaustion or intoxication is not an excuse for acts of poor character.* You are still responsible for your actions, regardless. One tip is to alert a friend or colleague of your condition and have them help you avoid getting into a bad situation. Another tool would be to have a trigger, like a visible bracelet, as a reminder to consider what you are about to do or say. The best tip I can offer here is to avoid getting yourself into an impaired state in the first place when you are representing the organization.

- **Rehearse before you say it or do it:** Observe the situation or interaction you are engaged in and pay attention to your gut reaction. Run scenarios and outcomes in your head until you are comfortable with the results.

Below are some attributes that apply to Excellence in Integrity. While these are not intended to replace what you have already established as your set of principles, there is a good chance they may reiterate or support those. You want to share, acknowledge, and reward these attributes to help build an environment conducive to implementing principles and maintaining a culture of Excellence in Integrity.

Integrity Attributes

Accessible: Committing time to be available to those who would value your attention.

Appreciative: Recognizing and acknowledging generosity or grace being shown to you.

Attentive: Focusing on a situation or person you have committed time to without being distracted.

Compliant: Understanding the value of order, structure, and rules, and working within those parameters.

Courageous: Setting aside fear to take decisive action in unknown or potentially perilous circumstances.

Courteous: Demonstrating good manners, even in emotional or confrontational situations.

Dependable: Showing consistent behavior that allows others to extend trust and confidence.

Discreet: Refraining from speaking, taking action, or exercising rights to protect private or sensitive information.

Generous: Giving abundantly of your resources to help meet others' needs.

Grace: Generously showing compassion or forgiveness without personal consideration.

Gracious: Expressing goodwill or hospitality to others whether it is earned or not.

Honest: Presenting the whole truth in a timely manner regardless of consequences.

Honorable: Upholding all others' positions, principles, and dignity with the highest respect within the boundaries of your principles.

Humble: Suppressing attention on yourself in order to focus attention on the appropriate people or situation.

Mentor: Serving as an advocate, guide, counselor, or instructor for the benefit and development of others.

Patient: Letting the investment in planning, preparation, and trust run its course.

Prudent: Being careful and responsible in managing your responsibilities.

Reasonable: Guided by reason or sensibility to refrain from erratic and emotional decisions or actions.

Restrained: Controlling impulses or reactions that run counter to a set of values or decorum.

Sincere: Demonstrating genuine actions and words consistent with beliefs and feelings.

Steadfast: Holding firm to your position, values, or commitments regardless of personal challenges.

Wise: Demonstrating discernment and good judgment in regard to the situation, people, and facts.

One last thought:

There are many reasons why it is important to have integrity and character in the culture of an organization, but a key one often overlooked is that people are happier in such a culture. How do you feel when you are around someone who supports high integrity and has good character? How do others feel around them?

Notes and Insights:

_____

_____

_____

_____

_____

_____

_____

_____

_____

_____

_____

_____

_____

_____

_____

_____

_____

_____

_____

_____

_____

_____

_____

_____

_____

CHAPTER 16:
EXCELLENCE IN CAPACITY

VISION HAS NO BOUNDARIES, BUT capacity dictates your plans. Leaders can easily mistake their vision for their plans. You may want your company to have the highest market share in your industry, but you need to make sure you have a viable plan based on available capacity to make that happen. Otherwise it is just bluster, which can harm the culture. In the roles defined in the Focus Phase of FEED Leader there is a progression through the Visionary Role, Strategist Role, and then the Planner Role. This is because there is a process to make your vision actionable, and it is dependent on understanding the capacity of your organization.

Excellence in Capacity is a broad concept that I generally define as having the right people in the right positions with the right resources to succeed. In essence, it is your organization's ability to produce. Linda spends a significant amount of her time training and developing others. She speaks to groups ranging from just a handful to crowds of more than 18,000, and she always incorporates motivation, belief, and purpose. However, she likes to be known as a "nuts and bolts" speaker; she wants people to leave her talks with actionable items that will help them to be better at their job. She wants them to have an expanded capacity.

Everyone in a leadership position wants to have quality output from their organization. Of course, this requires effort to set up your organization for success. *A function of leadership is to consistently expand what an organization is capable of doing.* When capacity is expanding, teams can face challenges with confidence and authority. This chapter will explore how leadership can expand the capacity of an organization and where leaders should spend their energy to develop Excellence in Capacity.

Leadership First

When Teak Leadership Group works with sales organizations, our approach is to work with the company's leadership first, the sales management second, and finally, the sales force. When there is a disconnect between how the sales force is selling and the organization's actual capacity, you risk poor service, employee strife, and customer dissatisfaction.

This disconnect happens more than you might think. I have found friction between the sales force and corporate in several organizations. I stress to both groups how critical it is to communicate throughout the organization on core capacity. It is crucial that the leadership set expectations within the *realities of capacity*. Reflect on what it means to be an "Triple A" Leader – Awareness, Anticipation, and Accountability, specifically in this regard. If you are *Aware* of your capacity's limits, *Anticipate* the dynamics, and are *Accountable* for the current level of capacity, you'll have a much easier time communicating and setting expectations. On the other hand, it's very difficult to expand capacity if you don't start with a realistic perspective.

Push the Limits

While being realistic, however, great leaders are motivating the organization to push their limits of capacity. In most businesses, it's hard to compete with others if you're not getting everything out of the resources you have. However, there is a difference between a boss pushing the limits and a leader pushing the limits.

> If you expect a lot from your organization, then your organization is going to expect a lot from you.

The analogy I use for this can be seen in football. It's frustrating to watch a football game when the coach is repeatedly calling the same play and it isn't working. Sometimes a boss can be like the football coach who keeps "running up the middle" unsuccessfully, then admonishing his team for not being tough enough. Coaches want to prove that their front linemen are tougher than the other team's, so they keep running the running back through the middle.

A leader, however, is the coach who may also be admonishing the team on their toughness all the while subtly tweaking the play, adjusting the personnel, or implementing a strategy to clear the way for the runner. If you expect a lot from your organization, then your organization is going to expect a lot from you. You need to expend energy clearing the way for success.

Whether you're already in or preparing yourself for a leadership position, there is probably a place in your story where you had to reach deep inside and put in extraordinary effort to excel against the odds. This is our focus on Personal Achievement in personal growth. Hopefully, you can recall times when you found a way to distinguish yourself. This can help you in two distinct ways. First, you need to draw from these experiences because it takes more energy than you might think to prepare others for success. Second, you'll need to draw from these experiences to relate to the expectations you set for members of your organization. Leadership has a lot less to do with *telling* others how to succeed, and a lot more to do with *showing* them how to succeed.

People tend to look at their leaders as experts. Linda and several others who have succeeded in her business often get the question: "What did you do to get where you are?" Successful people are perceived as experts in the business because they achieved things that others want to achieve. A leader's capacity for success drives the organization's capacity for success in the same way that a leader's character drives the organization's integrity. If you can find the successes in your story and use them to expand capacity in your organization, people will find it resonates. Even better is when you can cite the successes of other individuals in your organization and leverage *them* to expand organizational capacity. This shows a culture of success. Tell these stories often.

Linda is one of the top income earners in her company, but she is noted for her failures early on. She tells the story often where she achieved a promotion, then lost it, multiple times. She persisted and eventually achieved great success. The qualities she used to finally succeed are the same qualities her team needs to learn and understand will eventually lead to success, especially if they have had setbacks.

As you grow your capacity, you can use what you learned with Clarity, Belief, and Action to help the organization reach that "next level." As we discussed with Debrief Phase, hopefully in six months or a year from now you are not talking about the same capacity issues you currently talk about.

Capacity Segments

As an analyst, I like to chop up information, segment it, and organize it for better consumption. When I look at the leader's role in expanding capacity, I consider six segments of focus. The interesting thing about these segments is that each requires a different skillset. Not all leaders need to be experts in every segment, but it's important to surround yourself with people competent in each. (Hint: You will see a lot of concepts here that are executed with FEED Leader.)

1. **Objective:** To understand how to expand capacity, you must first understand what you are trying to accomplish. Keep the focus on what success looks like for the organization. Sometimes organizations get caught up in activities that don't support the core objective. They spend energy, time, and money on things that someone else is doing or that seem glamorous. Remember your purpose, and let that drive your objective. Sticking to an objective can be highly motivating to an organization. Any changes in direction must be very well thought out so as not to be a distraction.

2. **Planning:** Everything that happens after you've solidified an objective needs to be part of the plan. How do you get the right people in the right position with the right resources? You know whom you are looking for, what positions you need, and what resources are required. You might get lucky enough to experience some success without a plan; however, long-term, sustainable success requires some sort of blueprint. If this isn't present, you really don't know what success looks like, and thus your organization won't know what success looks like.

3. **Infrastructure:** I spoke at the beginning of the book about how I was a natural follower when I was younger. It didn't even occur to me to try to lead. I never openly questioned how things were going to happen. It wasn't until I owned a company that I realized for the first time that if *I* did not set something up to happen, then it probably was not going to happen. Infrastructure is an important consideration, and one that is easily overlooked. Infrastructure includes "structural" items such as communication, systems, data storage, data flow, equipment, facilities, analytical processes, and physical movement.

   Take the time in your planning process to understand where people are physically and how they move, interact, and share ideas; how resources are stored, moved, used, and replenished; how information is created, analyzed, stored, and shared; how products are created, stored, and moved.

   Importantly, consider the maximum capacity of each aspect of infrastructure, and which aspects limit your infrastructure. To illustrate simply, if you have the capacity to create 100 widgets a day but can only store 75 of those widgets, then storage is limiting your capacity to only create 75 widgets a day. Always lead within your capacity, and work to expand that capacity before increasing expectations on your organization. In other words, don't expect beyond what you provide. Don't expect someone to do research on the web if you don't provide access to Wi-Fi.

   I worked with an organization where the top leadership could not understand why they were having trouble penetrating a new market. The sales team tried to explain that they needed to have a bigger presence and investment in marketing and promotion to warm up the market. And yet, any request to invest in promotions was always declined. Then, a few weeks later the same issue would arise again. There was much frustration during this period. If there is a conflict between infrastructure and expectations, the onus is on leadership to resolve the conflict. Either develop the infrastructure or tamper down expectations.

4. **Resources:** Resources are the tools you use to do your work. I have spent a great deal of my career working with sales organizations. Some have been very sophisticated, others far less so. The more sophisticated organizations provide their salespeople with well-researched and well-developed resources. Sales people have an interesting position, since they are on the frontline of the organization. They are the first to make contact with their market, and most of the time, they experience some type of rejection or apathy.

Salespeople depend on resources to help them communicate and demonstrate their organization's products or services. One surefire way to disgruntle a salesperson is to send him or her out into the market ill prepared. And while this starts in sales, it extends to everyone in the organization. Resources need to be well thought out and used efficiently as part of the plan; more importantly, they must always be available.

In regard to Infrastructure and Resources, it is dangerous for a leader to make assumptions. Validate and verify things are in place for your organization to succeed. Teach your organization to validate and verify. *Be responsive and gracious when people question if things are in place.*

5. **Placement:** You need to understand what jobs need to be done, *then* find the right people to do them. Be purposeful and consistent in your plan for placing your people. Begin by determining what positions are required to accomplish your goals, and then put qualified people in those positions. Understand the difference between temporary and long-term needs. Good leaders will know there will need to be some adjustments, because it is rare that you will find exact skillsets required for each position. But if you have a good plan, it will be clear where and when you need to make adjustments.

One thing you hear about the perennial NFL Championship contenders (love them or hate them), the New England Patriots, is that they are a plug-and-play team. They always seem to have the key personnel in the right positions to succeed. One idea that their coach, Bill Belichick, espouses, is "do your job," and sometimes that job is not the same job a player had last week. It all depends on the needs. They don't always look for the superstar; just the person who will do their job!

What is important about this from a leadership standpoint is that it takes effort to be a FEED Leader. It takes concerted effort to know exactly what skills and talents you need and to evaluate candidates to put into those positions. Then you must train and equip them to fill those roles while mitigating their egos and previous habits. Then you must observe and evaluate performance for consistency and drive. Finally, you must invest time giving feedback and understanding their perspective. It is much easier to try and find the ace or superstar and ride their coattails. *But it doesn't lead to consistent success, or a sustainable culture of success.*

The goal for the leader is to continually be looking to make all their positions productive. Sometimes, this requires shifting personnel or responsibilities. As organizations increase capacity, there will be changes in the placement of their members.

6. **Training:** I encourage leaders to think of training as constant communication. After you have spent a great deal of energy in setting your objective, developing a plan, building your infrastructure, preparing your resources, and placing your people, it is time to *let your people know* about everything you have done. Continual training is necessary for growing capacity, because people must always be improving and staying current on industry trends, skills and knowledge.

I chose the following attributes for the Excellence in Capacity principle of the EPIC Construct. As you study these terms, imagine yourself and everyone on your team improving ten, twenty, or fifty percent for each attribute, and the difference that would make to the organization's Excellence in Capacity. For instance, a twenty percent improvement in diligence means fewer mistakes, higher quality, and increased efficiency.

To really understand the impact of growing these attributes, I recommend the following exercise. Take each word and list the benefits of a twenty percent or greater growth in that attribute in your people. Discuss this with your team and determine practical ways to make that happen. This exercise is designed to allow everyone to feel the full potential of each attribute. These attributes reflect an environment conducive to implementing good practices to expand Excellence in Capacity.

Capacity Attributes

Adaptable: Making appropriate adjustments to meet the needs of dynamic situations.

Aware: Being alert to circumstances and people in order to be prepared.

Compelling: Providing a force in influencing actions and behaviors to accomplish objectives.

Competent: Having the skills and aptitude to fulfill responsibilities.

Decisive: Making timely, resolute decisions backed by your full authority.

Diligent: Constantly attentive to details required to accomplish an objective regardless of distractions.

Effort: Applying appropriate physical or mental energy to accomplish work.

Efficient: Being most productive while expending the least amount of resources.

Enterprising: Willing to take on new, important, or difficult projects with great enthusiasm and ingenuity.

Initiative: Being the first to take appropriate action.

Innovative: Inserting new ideas or perspectives.

Orderly: Maintaining organization and discipline to a system.

Persistent: Moving forward despite opposition, obstacles, or discouragement.

Punctual: Adhering to a schedule or deadline.

Thorough: Providing complete, detailed, and accurate work while exhausting possible detractions.

One last thought:

There is a lot of pride in an organization with a high capacity to succeed. As a leader, set up a culture where it seems like you always have good news: "we exceeded our revenue goals," "we have new and improved tools to work with," "we have the highest retention rate," "we have new and exciting products coming out," and so on.

Notes and Insights:

_____
_____
_____
_____
_____
_____
_____
_____
_____
_____
_____
_____
_____
_____
_____
_____
_____
_____
_____
_____
_____
_____
_____
_____
_____
_____

CHAPTER 17:
EPIC CULTURE IN A REAL ORGANIZATION

I DEVELOPED EPIC WHILE OBSERVING and working with Linda. However, I realized afterwards that I had a glimpse of the principles of EPIC during my time in the corporate world. There was a time at Merck when our leaders put a lot of effort into building belief. For several years, I worked in a culture that bred success, and year after year, across the board, we met or exceeded expectations. There was an environment of very high employee commitment to our division. Some of us were contacted several times by headhunters to fill positions at other companies, often for more money or with a promotion. But it was rare to see anyone leave.

I remember, however, a friend at Merck who was going through a period of frustration. He was having trouble landing a position he desired within the company. Though he had been promoted a few times, he wanted something closer to his home state. He took a job at another company for a promotion and more money near his home. Soon, he was telling his close friends that he was missing the Merck environment and cautioning others not to leave.

EPIC Culture

When I think back to our leadership, I visualize leaders who built **Excellence in Purpose**. They were *Engaging* in that they interacted with us like they had been in our shoes and were interested in our success. And there was good reason for this: for the most part, our executives *had* held similar positions to ours before their ascent. They were *Insightful* in their understanding of where we were and what we needed to succeed. We believed in our purpose and felt confident that our leadership knew how to guide us towards success. I would not say they were completely transparent, but they kept us *Focused* on our jobs. They kept us from being distracted by what could be or what others were doing in the market that was not the way we were going. They showed *Conviction* in the things that made us great, and they cultivated that conviction in us. The leaders encouraged innovation, but also constantly reminded us of who we were and what made us successful.

Our purpose was reinforced by our leadership's desire that we grow **Excellence in Integrity**. It was common for our leaders to tell us to judge everything we did by this standard: "act as if everything you do is going to be on the front page of the *Wall Street Journal*" (or the *New York Times* or *USA Today*). Our *Compliance* with industry and company standards was not only expected; we were continuously tested on our knowledge and understanding of these standards. And we were constantly coached on using *Discretion* in interacting with coworkers and customers. Time and again we heard that doing the right thing takes precedence over saving money, completing an objective, or getting a sale. Our leadership was also *Reasonable* in considering our opinions, no matter our position.

My first position in the corporate office was as an analyst working on a high-impact, high-profile negotiation. I did research and developed reports for the negotiating team as we put together our proposal. When it was time to present to the executive group for final approval, I was invited to the meeting to provide support materials as needed. We were all sitting around a large conference table. At the conclusion of the presentation, the Vice President of Sales said that he wanted complete buy-in on the proposal. He wanted to make sure *everyone* was satisfied and that there were no outstanding concerns.

Then he did something that surprised me, something I remember to this day: he went around the table and had every person voice their support or dissent for the proposal. I was packing up my materials when I noticed complete silence in the room. The account executive I had been working with tapped my leg. I looked up and everybody was staring at me. I had broken out in a cold sweat, but I confidently voiced my approval of the proposal, and the Vice President continued canvassing the room. I had assumed that either my voice didn't matter or that it was assumed that I approved. That Vice President modeled an important lesson: that regardless of one's position, everyone has a voice. It was a little thing, but I felt respected.

I developed a great understanding for the impact that integrity has on the culture. Before I started working for Merck, I came from an industry with an environment in which what I was "supposed to do" was not always consistent with what was actually done. In my prior profession, I'd found myself pressured to do things because that was what everyone else was doing. As I learned about the actual standards, I had trouble reconciling that with some decisions I was making. It was even awkward to follow the desired behavior at times, because it put me at odds with what my peers expected me to do. There was such inconsistency between procedures and behavior that even some of those who were supposed to enforce policies advised me to counter those policies. It was such a contrast to my later experience at Merck.

It was refreshing working in an organization that appreciated compliance and where there were no "unwritten rules" on how we were supposed to *actually* act. Not only was there a culture of highly motivated and committed individuals; they had a reputation for quality output. Training and coaching were consistently employed to make sure we distinguished ourselves in the market. They strived for **Excellence in Capacity**.

I noticed that our customers and other stakeholders had a high regard for our products and our relationships with them. It all started with recruiting, hiring, and promoting highly *Competent* people. Not only did the leadership exhibit an *Enterprising* spirit, they also had encouraged the organization to be enterprising as well. Because we were a high-profile and a premier company in the industry, there were high expectations to be met. As a member of the organization, I always had extreme confidence that challenges would be met in a way that helped the organization thrive.

I remember having discussions with colleagues during a time when it seemed every conference call or meeting brought good news. Leadership was always working on *Innovative* products, projects, and initiatives that would benefit our organization. They modeled and rewarded *Persistent* and *Diligent* behavior that expanded our capacity to get work done. They also modeled and rewarded *Awareness* to ideas and circumstances that would reduce distractions and make us more productive. We had a lot of confidence in our leadership and our organization. We were always reminded of our founder's sentiment that when we focus on providing the best for society, customers will come, and profits follow.

While the specifics of EPIC weren't apparent to me then, they certainly are now when I think about it. We were clear about our purpose at Merck: saving lives and enabling customers to provide good products to their patients. This awareness drove the motivation to do things ethically and with integrity, and to increase our capacity to do good work. Maintaining *high integrity* is consistent with *purpose*, and builds the character needed to maintain a *high capacity*. In turn, having a *high capacity* to produce great products and serve our customers well reinforces *purpose* and rewards *integrity*. Leaders focusing on Excellence in Purpose, Integrity, and Capacity will generate a self-nourishing cycle that generates a Culture of Success.

Culture Needs Maintenance to Thrive

Unfortunately, when you stop developing Purpose, Integrity, and Capacity, the cycle can diminish over time. Not long before I took a management position and then later decided to resign to consult for Linda in her business full time, there was turnover at Merck's corporate offices at the highest level. Though much of what I share about what happened next is based on my personal observations and chatter, the effects were palpable. Top executives were forced to leave the company, and almost overnight we could feel the changes.

Soon, new leaders were brought in from other divisions. They talked about maintaining the successful culture there; however, culture develops from a deep-seated belief, long-standing traditions, and established behavior. The new leadership had none of that and lacked the patience to adapt. They eventually relied on remnants of their previous culture. Gone were many of the things that made our division's culture great.

I remember a significantly impactful meeting of all the corporate employees in our division after the executive shakeup. An executive started talking about stock prices, earnings, analyst reports, and the decisions made based on all of these. Long-term strategic projects were shuttered to devote resources to meet analysts' expectations. Pending reorganization, layoffs, and budget cuts were discussed.

To this point, my colleagues and I had been inundated with messages of benefitting society, serving our customers, high performance of our division, and long-term strategies. Our leadership had never labored over analyst projections or stock movement; they knew we were not a quarterly business. Our marketing initiatives and product development were generally multiyear processes. Besides that, we were getting ready to launch several new promising products and we were ready to ramp up, not cut back.

I cherish and appreciate my time with the company, and I really enjoyed all the jobs I had there. Merck is still a great company that has experienced success over the last decade, and my time there truly helped me realize that a culture—no matter how well established—needs constant attention. If the new leaders had taken the time to try and emulate the Purpose of why we did what we did, if they had emphasized the importance of our Integrity, and built Capacity instead of limited it, they probably could have maintained that Culture of Success that so many had worked so hard to create.

After I left Merck, I heard stories from some of my old colleagues who were experiencing success and getting recognition in their new positions in other divisions. They would tell me that all they were doing was implementing the principles they had learned under the old culture—and everybody told them how great it was.

Culture of success can be created within any organization over time. You can create a culture of success from your position within your area of influence, and success is contagious. Focus on Excellence in Purpose, Integrity, and Capacity, and people will notice and want to join that Culture of Success.

One last thought:
The Leader Legacy is about building cultural equity in your organization. Take some time to imagine what your organization would look like if it demonstrated excellence in purpose, excellence in integrity, and excellence in capacity. What would your legacy be with that organization?

Notes and Insights:

_____

_____

_____

_____

_____

_____

_____

_____

_____

_____

_____

_____

_____

_____

_____

_____

_____

_____

_____

_____

_____

_____

_____

_____

_____

_____

WRAP-UP

It's time! When you look in the mirror you should see a leader. Start by leading yourself based on your vision and passion. People will notice and start to look to you for leadership. Then, look and act like a leader by understanding your roles and actions in those roles. Finally, spread your influence throughout your organization.

CHAPTER 18:
A LEADER IN THE MIRROR

I HAVE WORKED WITH MANY leaders and experienced many cultures in my career. What intrigues me about the people in Linda's organization is how happy and fulfilled they are. They are a vivacious, generous, caring, and gracious group of people. Several of us in this business would often comment how nice it would have been to have this culture in our previous work experiences. Is it possible to have this culture in the traditional corporate world? Yes! And it is all determined by leadership.

The CBA (Clarity, Belief, and Action) for personal growth, the FEED Leader process (Focus, Equip, Execute, and Debrief) for developing ourselves as leaders, and the EPIC Construct (Excellence in Purpose, Integrity, and Capacity) for spreading influence in an organization with a Culture of Success are tools designed to help leaders develop a culture like the one that Linda's organization has been working in for over a decade. As you implement these tools, you will see yourself as an effective leader. I wrote earlier about putting yourself mentally in a place of success and looking around to help understand how you got there. We enjoy a sense of fulfillment, not from *arriving* at success, but rather from the *experience* of doing what it takes to achieve success and growing from there. Personal Character, Personal Fulfillment, and Personal Achievement keep progressing—so our satisfaction comes from our growth, not a fixed point of having "arrived." I have become passionate about finding ways to help leaders not only be successful, but also to create a work environment where people thrive and are fulfilled in their journey.

At Merck, we were constantly reminded of our founder George W. Merck's statement: *"We try to remember that medicine is for the patient. We try never to forget that medicine is for the people. It is not for the profits. The profits follow, and if we have remembered that, they have never failed to appear. The better we have remembered it, the larger they have been."*

What if our conversations within our organization emphasized our value to the community instead of profits and growth? What if we are focused on personal character, personal fulfillment, and personal achievement in our organizations instead of income or ego? What if leaders throughout organizations respected their teams and focused on each member's individual success and well-being instead of how their teams will glorify them? If we allow these values to define our organizations, then the profits, growth, monetary reward, influence, and leadership recognition will come. This is all possible; we just need good leaders to make it happen.

Will you be one of those leaders? It doesn't matter what your position is right now. Realizing the leader in you will take you farther than you can comprehend. I have realized throughout my own journey that it's all a matter of what you are bold enough to envision. I have a big, hopeful vision for the leader you can become.

> *Whatever your successes and failures, God is ready to use you right now.*

Linda shares something with her organization that I want to share with you. "You are worthy!" God made you worthy. It's not your degree, age, experience, connections, money, or situation that makes you worthy. Whatever your successes and failures, God is ready to use you right now. Start by leading yourself. Are you willing to grow personally? As a leader? As an organization?

Can you see a leader in the mirror?

This is the most crucial question to answer, for others will see you the way you project yourself. Don't look around and compare yourself to others. Don't define who you are by the way others might label you. We are each unique and have something special to offer. You have way more potential than you can fathom, so don't let anything limit your vision.

It is good to be part of a larger vision. Take time to describe what success looks like for you, and don't think small. Don't get bogged down with the idea that "there is no way I can make it there from here." Remember, you want to work from a perspective where you have already achieved your vision.

There was a period of time where all I could do was drive to the local park, study my Bible, and pray. I didn't know what to do or where to go. I was overwhelmed with feelings that everyone was disappointed in me and that people were looking for me because I owed them something. Success to me was just finding a reason to go somewhere besides the park. Success was finding the courage to find out how bad things really were, so I could start developing a plan. Success was just getting some income, so I could know we would have a place to live and food for my young family.

I had to be a leader for myself and my family. I had to constantly expand what success was to me. I started dreaming of paying off our debt, working on a new career, and then thriving. What I noticed was that the bigger I dreamed, the more I believed in that dream, and the more actions I took towards that dream, the more people took interest and joined me. As I cultivated my character and looked for fulfillment versus existence, I began to accumulate achievements. The more I achieved, the more people looked to me to lead. As I started to take on more formal leadership roles, I started developing the basis for leadership principles like CBA, FEED Leader, and EPIC. It is to God's glory that I am now in a position to help others see the leader in themselves and help them be successful.

What does success look like to me now? Over the years, I've been blessed to travel the world with Linda and with family and friends. We've been to several countries and experienced countless cultures, visited beautiful exotic islands, and cruised the Atlantic, Pacific, Caribbean, and the Fjords of Norway. We've built our dream house on a beautiful, wooded, two-acre lot. We've had the freedom to live anywhere we want.

Is that my picture of success? Nope! That is not what I am picturing.

We have been blessed, for sure; but my picture of success was and remains something different. It has more to do with family, service, bonding with friends, enjoying our work, and striving to glorify God in everything we do. The travels we have enjoyed are more about family adventures (and some of them were quite adventuresome), quality time with friends, and enjoying God's creation. The house we built means so much to me because we designed it as a family and considered how we can use it to serve. We made sure to have room to host church youth activities, have sleepovers, accommodate our large families, and enjoy dinner parties with old and new friends.

We decided to move close to family so Linda and I could see our brothers and sisters more often and the kids could spend time with their cousins. We wanted to spend time with our parents in their golden years and give "grandparent time" to our kids. It was a blessing to be close when my mother was diagnosed and succumbed to cancer, so we could spend time talking, laughing, and singing with her and the family in the waning weeks of her life.

The most rewarding endeavor, however, is the experience we had in spending time and money to help others. There is nothing like seeing a child develop a heart of giving and serving. We tried to teach our children about leadership; we don't hold back in letting them know about all the hours and effort that goes on behind the scenes—the strength it takes to help others in times of need or uncertainty. Their hearts are tender and their spirits giving. The little girl who I had no idea how I was going to support twenty years ago gave a moving valedictorian speech at her graduation. The little boy who wants the best for everyone he knows, even someone who makes the game-winning shot against his team. Sarah and Preston are the most tender-hearted, generous, and faith-based people I know.

That is *my* picture of success.

Success isn't based on accomplishments; what matters is how we influence and improve things for others. Success is based on how you feel at the end of the day. Success is based on the environment we put ourselves in, including the effect we had on others. It doesn't matter what we have and have not done if others don't become better in the process. I was not sure what skills I had to offer when I was looking to rebuild my life, but I became confident I could help others. I focused on serving others and that developed my leadership skills, which was the main thing I needed to develop to move ahead.

I was coaching an employee for a client a few years ago. The client called me in for a meeting and expressed disappointment in how the coaching was going, which surprised me because I had thought it was going very well. I couldn't imagine what the problem was. The client was upset because the employee was talking about the leadership skills he was developing. The client did not see this person as a leader because he didn't have anyone reporting to him. They thought I was filling his head with big ideas about his future. I asked if his relationship with his manager was improving. "Yes." I asked if his relationship with coworkers was improving. Again, "yes." I asked if he was being more proactive and contributing in a more positive way. "Yes," he was.

I certainly *hope* I was filling his head with big ideas. I hope he inspired others to have big ideas as well. We can lead from any position—and when we do, opportunities will find us.

> *We can lead from any position— and when we do, opportunities will find us.*

Don't give up, because—take it from me—there are big things ahead. Keep the engine running. Let the Glory of God rise up among you. Tell your story and be an inspiration to others. That person you see in the mirror every day is the most important leader in your life. Be that Leader!

One last thought:
Do you want to see the leader in you? Go back through all the chapters and look at the notes you made. These notes on what you thought were important and hopefully were your first impressions. I think you will be impressed with what you were thinking and the actions you want to take to be a better leader. God Bless!

To order books or for information on bulk orders
Visit www.teakleader.com
You can also find updates on events and
support materials for "A Leader in the Mirror"
on our website.